All My Born Days

All My Born Days

◆

Stories by a Sharecropper's Son

Historical autobiography

Kenneth R. Shipe

iUniverse, Inc.
New York Lincoln Shanghai

All My Born Days
Stories by a Sharecropper's Son

iUniverse, Inc.

For information address:
iUniverse, Inc.
2021 Pine Lake Road, Suite 100
Lincoln, NE 68512
www.iuniverse.com

ISBN: 0-595-28795-6 (pbk)
ISBN: 0-595-74886-4 (cloth)

Printed in the United States of America

Contents

List Of Photographs

Acknowledgements

To my Dad, John Russell Shipe, who never owned land or had a bank account or graduated from a school, but knew the rhythm of the seasons and how to make the soil produce to sustain his family and farm animals. He taught me to read the codes of the soil handed down from generation to generation: secrets of when to till, to plant, to cultivate, to harvest, how to preserve the bounty of the harvest, and trim the vineyards and orchards for the next growing season.

To my Mom, Pearl Amanda Shipe, who arose first each day, started the fires in the stoves, prepared the wonderful meals, mended and washed our clothes, milked the cows, and fed the chickens. She was Santa and Easter Bunny. She knew the things that pleased God and wanted those things in my life; I heard her prayers and observed God answer her petitions. She was the last to bed at night after the fires were safely banked in the stoves.

To Mrs. Helen Miller, who drove me back and forth to school in her personal car off Martins Mountain each day for two-years. She encouraged me to discuss important current events with her. Her many acts of kindness toward my Mom are a daily reminder to me to stretch myself to reach out to help others.

To Mrs. Alice Harris, my fifth grade teacher, who knew how to motivate me to work to my full potential in school. My classmates called me her pet; I knew she loved me and that's all that mattered.

To Russ Burbank, my good friend, who had to muster every ounce of his Harvard education and his many years of editorial and writing experience to edit my twisted prose. He allowed me to write in my childhood voice, one without eloquence, to tell my story.

To Dottie, my wife and love of my life for fifty years. She maneuvered her way through our motorcoach strewn with computers, scanners, printers, CD burners and endless entanglements of wire on the floor for three years while I wrote. She proofread my text. She also knows the language that God likes and she held an imaginary plumb bob over the text to keep the manuscript on plumb vertically.

Foreword

You might say that this book began one evening in the laundry room of a campground near Orlando, when my wife Carol and I were doing our biweekly wash and met another couple engaged in the same mundane pursuit. The four of us began chatting about an unmatched black sock and established that it belonged to Carol, then the conversation moved on to the usual retiree staples: Where you from? Where've you been? What did you do for work before you retired?

It appeared to Carol and me that these were friendly people with whom we had some things in common. They were about the same age and liked many of the things we liked, such as traveling the United States in what the public knows as recreational vehicles but a lot of us roamers utilize as actual houses on wheels.

Soon the wash was done. Ken and Dottie Shipe invited us back to their motorcoach for ice cream and we continued our conversation. Ken told us he had retired a few years ago from a big aerospace corporation, where he had supervised the launching of 21 space vehicles. He talked a little about his boyhood, living on a back road farm in West Virginia and growing up during the Depression without amenities such as electricity, running water and a bathroom. Dottie told how she and Ken had raised two sons and two daughters while moving around the country to jobsites that ranged from launching pads in Cape Canaveral to missile silos in Colorado, Wyoming, Iowa, Nebraska and California. Carol shared how she had been an elementary school teacher for 32 years and I told some yarns about the 42 years I had spent as a reporter and editor for newspapers and magazines. We exchanged postal and e-mail addresses, and said we'd keep in touch.

The next day Ken and Dottie left to travel northward in their luxurious motorcoach, in which they have lived year-round since they grew bored with the view at the mountain home they had built in Colorado after Ken retired. They had sold their log house, moved into a motorcoach and gone traveling, crisscrossing the nation at will, going north in summer and south in winter, visiting family and friends as they moved from one place to another.

Over the next few months the Shipes kept us up to date about their meanderings by means of e-mail and a newsletter, *Tumbleweeds*, which Ken produced occasionally on his laptop computer. Heading to Newfoundland that next summer, they paused at a campground in Massachusetts and we stopped by to visit them. The next day they came to our house in Sagamore Beach and we gave them a half-day tour of Cape Cod. Our paths have crossed many times since as Carol and I leave home each winter and spend time in the South, at many of the same campgrounds that Ken and Dottie favor.

During one of those winter encounters Ken mentioned that he would like to write a book about his family history and growing up on a sharecropper farm. I'd heard a lot of his tales and knew that they could be really good reading, so I urged him to get going at it. And I volunteered to be the editor. Little did we know, as the saying goes, what we were getting into, how large a task we were undertaking. Over the next three years Ken typed out first one chapter then another, and the number of pages stored in his computer grew ever so slowly. He would e-mail each chapter to me as he completed it, and I would go over the words, sometimes straightening out sentence structure or rearranging some of the paragraphs. I'd e-mail him questions and he would send back the answers. Back and forth the words would go, over the Internet.

Once in a while during our winter meetings we would talk about genealogy. Ken had done a considerable amount of studying and knew that his ancestors had come to America from Germany sometime during the 1700s, but his research had come to a dead end. I had a paper left by a long-departed aunt that said one of my mother's ancestors had come from the Palatine section of Germany, and I wanted to learn more. So one night we four decided: "Let's go to Germany together." We made plans, communicating by e-mail and telephone until travel arrangements finally were completed.

Ken and Dottie came to our house in October 2000 and we boarded a plane in Boston that took us to Paris. Sharing a leased car we traveled 2,100 miles in a 23-day tour of Western Europe. One of our first stops was at the Palatine registry in Kaiserslautern, Germany, where I learned that my ancestor was not on the passenger list of any vessel that had transported Palatines to the New World. (Later I learned that my aunt had been wrong; all my ancestors came over from England.) Ken, however, fared much better. The registry pointed him to the town of Odernheim am Glan, which we reached the next day. We arrived shortly after noon and Carol and I headed down the main street to a small market to buy snacks, since we had skipped lunch. When we walked back up the street we saw Ken and Dottie in the middle of a group of people. Ken had found some Shipes and a woman named Uta Weaver, who had spent several years in the United States and spoke good English. The crowd was getting ready to uncork a bottle of eight-day-old wine to honor their newfound Shipe relatives. From what we could understand, much of the town's population was either a Shipe or a Shipe descendent. The townsfolk got glasses for Carol and me and we joined them in a toast. One of the girls left and came back with a book about Odernheim am Glan history dating back to ancient times. Uta took us in her van to the "new" burgomeister's house where Ken was able to purchase a copy. Then Uta brought us to the home of the "old" burgomeister, whose mother was a Shipe and who had piles of Shipe history on shelves in his dining room. Uta translated as he and Ken compared notes on their ancestors. When we left to continue our tour Ken was on top of the world. His visit to Odernheim am Glan was more than he had hoped for, and it provided a large part of the Shipe family history that he has included in the last chapter of this book.

Gradually, Ken's accumulation of chapters grew to a point where he had to think about how to end the book. Should it end when he reached high school? No, there was more that he wanted to tell. So he wrote recollections of his service in the Marines during the Korean War, enduring bitter cold, watching a flaming plane crash, riding in a fighter as it destroyed an enemy convoy at night, returning home a vastly different person than the Ken Shipe who had left, and then confronting the opportunity for a new kind of life that would transform a farm boy into an aerospace engineer.

The essential value of this book is rooted in Ken's ability to recall exact details of happenings during his boyhood. His extraordinary memory enabled him to provide names, dates, facts and descriptions that make his stories vivid and real. You will be with Ken atop a sled as it careens out of control down an icy hillside, beside him years later as a decrepit Model T loses its brakes and veers into a ditch on that same hillside, and trembling with him and his family as they hide terror-stricken under canvas while a forest fire sweeps over their farm. Ken will tell you how he felt when his pet calf went to the slaughterhouse, and will take you along on his first romantic encounters. He will introduce you to a neighbor woman who insisted that he get a good education and helped him do it.

Publishing a book is much like shooting an arrow in the air: it falls to earth you know not where (apologies to Longfellow). Whatever will happen to this particular book, I hope that copies find their way into homes, libraries, and historical societies in the vicinity of Cumberland, Maryland and nearby West Virginia. Ken has created an authentic record of the heroic people who wrested meager livings from the region's hills and valleys more than half a century ago, and he has written it from a perspective that probably no other author could achieve. For this he deserves the acclaim of local historians and others who want to know and preserve details from the region's past.

The essence of Ken's story is that in America, people may escape backgrounds of poverty and, through hard work and good fortune, climb high on the ladders of professional accomplishment. Ken Shipe was able to do that, and his story is enthralling. Thanks, Ken, for giving me a part in the telling.

Russ Burbank
May 2003

Preface

There is an imaginary line, the Eastern Continental Divide, which runs along the top of the Appalachian Mountains. The northern part of these mountains is known as the Alleghenies. These mountains formed a major barrier to migration of my ancestors and other westward bound early pioneers who chose to travel through the western regions of West Virginia, Maryland and Pennsylvania. This imaginary line determines the direction a raindrop will flow when it hits the ground. Raindrops that fall west of this line flow into the tributary streams of the Ohio Valley and eventually into the Mississippi River. Raindrops that fall east of the line will flow toward the tributaries of the Potomac River, either the north or south branch and then eventually into the Chesapeake Bay. There will always be someone who will contend that this distinction is unfair and may ask, suppose the drop splits the line? My answer is you have to trust God to take care of these matters and believe that He will cause the water to end up on the side He chooses.

Regardless of where you stand on this important issue, the drop begins where it begins and that's just a fact of raindrop life, and I believe the same holds true for people. Hence, we begin where we begin and as an individual we have no choice in the matter, nor do we have the right to challenge where we begin.

The question of splitting raindrops and which direction a life will go became relevant to me when I was shown a picture of my paternal grandfather's grave headstone by my nephew, Craig Shipe, and he asked, "Have you ever been to the grave?" I had to answer, "No." He said, "I have been to the farm graveyard once when I was young, but I don't believe I could find the graveyard again; I'd just like to return to pay a visit to my great-grandfather." At that moment my igno-rance of my forefathers and the realization of how I had neglected them pierced my heart. I had felt that since all four of my grandparents had died before I was born that somehow I had concluded that they weren't interested in knowing me; therefore, I had never given any thought to connecting with them. But because of this incident I became motivated to begin a quest to find my roots and write my story.

I am more than three score and ten years old at the time of this writing and I had steered clear of genealogists until now, but better late than never to learn the art of genealogy.

My family tree roots can be traced deep on both sides, paternal and maternal. Exploring those roots and the search for sources of information about my family roots pricked my inquisitive mind. From this research I found that my cousin, Paul David Shipe, has been doing genealogical research into the history of my mother's family and I obtained much of the information that I have included in this book from his unpublished manuscript, *The Gathering*. I learned that my ancestors' town of origin is Odernheim am Glan, County of Bad Kreusnach, Rheinland-Pfalz Territory, Germany. The small village of Odernheim am Glan is about 30 kilometers from the Rhein River, near the town of Bingen.

For my wife Dottie, and me, our family histories will never be the same for now we are comfortable with placing our ancestors right in the middle of the actions of historical events. After just a few short years, we are becoming genealogy researchers and both of our laptop files are filled with our family members in their proper relationship within the family tree. We are making strides in placing them in their proper historical timeframe. We have experienced the work of wrestling with heavy birth, death and marriage ledgers and land record books in courthouses, of climbing hills to find farm graveyards and trying to locate towns that no longer exist on maps. We have felt the pain when we had to throw away good socks that were so matted with beggar lice seeds that we couldn't afford the time away from our research to pick off the seeds.

We took a wonderful trip to Europe in the fall of 2000, sharing travel expenses and experiences with our friends, Russ and Carol Burbank of Cape Cod, who share our interest in genealogy and travel. We visited the city of the Scheib/ Shipe family's origin; Odernheim am Glan, Germany. We enjoyed that city with its beautiful old walls and entry gates, a balanced mixture of modern and ancient buildings, as well as, their important monuments. Some of the monuments were engraved with names of my family members. These locations now have a significant place in our minds. The people we met share a special place in our hearts.

My ancestors who lived in Odernheim am Glan are recorded in books written by the citizens of the town and they are traceable by Space Agers like us as far back as the Dark Ages. My ancestor's names are engraved on plaques, gravestones and monuments in the city. I am so proud of my forefathers and their families for what they achieved as well as of the present-day people in Odernheim am Glan who have dedicated themselves to preservation of our heritage.

We made a special visit to Kaiserslautern, Germany, and in the Institu fur Pfalzische GeschichteUnd Volkskunde, we had a 'goose bump' experience when we found listed the name of the Shipe family's original immigrant to America, Christian Scheib. His personal data was recorded in the index that listed all persons who migrated from the Palatinate area of Germany between 1700 and 1780, the period of major migration from this area to America.

I had the pleasure and honor to sit in the home of the former burgomeister of Odernheim am Glan, Karl Wenz, and to meet his lovely wife. He has been researching the Scheib family since 1937 and is one of the authors of the German language book; *Odernheim am Glan und Disibodenberg*. Coincidentally, Karl shared with me through an interpreter that we are related through his mother's side of his family. We found Karl to be a handsome and articulate octogenarian gentleman. Karl's research lists family members as early as the Dark Ages.

As continued research introduces me to my forefathers and their families, I learn of their trials, tribulations and triumphs. My discovery of their contributions to society within a historical framework has been one of the most rewarding experiences in all my born days.

My purpose in writing my story is twofold: First, to preserve a written record of my personal recollections, genealogy research and family remembrances of our sharecropping lifestyle in the 20th century in the Allegheny Mountains. Second, to encourage others to record some verbal descriptions befitting their own family name and to add substance to the skeletal framework of their family tree.

We are all historical survivors; hence we are a story waiting to be told. Some folks seem to be waiting for the proper life-event to occur, like a time of serenity or some other event. I'm not sure if I know what serenity means, or more important, whether serenity will ever occur. Start today.

1

Sharecropping in West Virginia

My mother, Pearl Amanda Shipe, was fifteen and a month when she met Dad, John Russell Shipe, at an orchard on Knobly Mountain near Keyser, West Virginia. She was working in the kitchen that fed the seasonal apple pickers and teamsters. Dad, 22, was a teamster hauling apples from the orchards to the railhead in Cumberland, Maryland. Dad owned a wagon, a team of four mules and some farming equipment. He also used his wagon and team to haul chestnut tree bark from the Appalachian and Allegheny Mountain high country to tanneries at Paw Paw and the Lost River area of West Virginia.

Mom and Dad were married August 10, 1910, in Cumberland, Maryland, and began housekeeping in a sharecropper's house on the Washington farms near Romney, Hampshire County, West Virginia. This farm is now a museum and visitors can conclude that the farm was originally designed to monitor work on the farm from a central point. The main house has a cupola on the third floor from which the overseer could view the activities of the entire farm.

My dad was called to report for service in World War I but he was sent home to take care of his young family because his right middle finger was permanently disfigured in a crescent shape due to a rattlesnake bite. The rattler bit him when he picked up a piece of bark to load onto his wagon. But the most critical health issue leading to his deferment from the Army was that he had a silver plate in his head the size of a silver dollar, the result of a riding accident as a child. A horse he was riding broke for the barn, and his head struck the top of the barn door.

In 1920, when Mom's mother, Samantha Lee Shipe, died, Mom was with her. Grandmother, 45 years old, had a cut on her leg that would not heal, and she contracted gangrene in the wound, which caused her death. My grandfather, John David Shipe, raised his remaining ten younger children with the help of my mom and dad, as well as, neighbors until he died of stomach problems in 1927. Friends and family raised his four youngest children after his death until they were grown.

On September 28, 1922, my dad's father, Lorenzo Dale Shipe, was killed in a train and truck crash in Broadway, Virginia. My paternal grandfather and another man died instantly, their bodies crushed by Southern Railway Passenger Train #12. Two other men survived the crash in critical condition. Due to the horrific condition of Lorenzo's remains, he was buried the next day in the Culler's family graveyard in the Dovesville section of the Lost River area near Mathias, West Virginia. Dad was not contacted in time to attend his father's funeral.

By 1923, my parents had six children: Clyde, born in 1911, Herbert in 1915, William in 1917, Lena in 1918, Betty in 1920 and Georgia in 1923. The family struggled as sharecroppers, and the river often flooded the land along the edge of the South Branch of the Potomac River where they lived.

In the 1920's, a Mr. Callahan offered Dad a sharecropper opportunity on his farm downstream from the Washington farm at a place the family called "The Bend," where the river widened, slowed and meandered in a large curve. My brother Jesse was born there in 1925.

The Washington and Roles families, black people, lived next door to us. The Roles had two daughters, Bea and Ally, who were best friends to my sisters, and often the girls spent the night at each other's homes. Ally died suddenly, and my family helped the Roles as much as they could to overcome their grief.

My dad found a part-time job driving a school bus in Hampshire County. His route included the areas of Five Points and Millison Mill. My brothers Clyde, Herbert and William and my sister, Lena attended the Parker one-room school-house. The Parker school, built in 1885, was near the family home at The Bend. When the school was closed in 1926 the kids went to school in Springfield, more than three miles distant. This school housed grades 1 through 8.

My family in 1923 at The Bend along the South Branch of the Potomac
River near Springfield, WV
L to r: Herbert, William, Clyde, Dad, holding Betty, Mom, holding
Georgia, and Lena

When the family lived at The Bend, they walked to services at a church in Springfield. The circuit-rider pastor preached there about one Sunday a month. After one service the preacher said to my dad, "It's bad enough that you live down there next to them niggers, but we believe you are too friendly with them and you're doing too much to help them, and God knows what else is going on." Hearing that, my dad vowed to never darken the church door again as long as he lived. Prior to the preacher's remarks, Dad had faithfully attended church. He had a Bible that was given to him by the church for perfect Sunday school attendance. The family said that after the accusations about his relationship with his black neighbors; he changed and began to curse, use tobacco and drink alcohol. He also was comfortable with mostly staying home.

After a while, Dad took employment at a railroad tie preservation plant in Green Spring, West Virginia. The tie plant treated green railroad, cross ties with creosote to preserve the wood. My uncle Clarence, who was married to Ella, my mom's sister, were partners in unloading the 500-pound green ties from railroad cars and loading the treated ties onto flatcars. The men were paid by the piece instead of an hourly wage.

Dad moved the family from the house at The Bend to Millison's Mill. Fresh water springs along the mountain provided water to the crick that ran near the house. The water in the crick was dammed, so that when it reached a certain depth, it spilled into a race. The water from the race ran in front of our log house on its way over the big wheel at the mill. At this house we had a hog pen, chicken house, garden, icehouse, spring house, root cellar, a place for cows, and a three-hole outhouse. A little bridge spanned the race, and a path from the house crossed this bridge to a dirt road. This road went by the house and in one direction it led you to Springfield or in the other direction along the river to a place called Five Points. At the end of the path from our house to the road, Dad had a roadside stand where he sold vegetables, melons and sweet corn and the like. Along the river were many cottages occupied during the summer by vacationers, mostly schoolteachers and other people that had means.

Three of my older brothers; Clyde, Herbert, who we called Tuck, and William, who we called Bill, were awakened at 1 a.m. on February 16, 1932, to ride the mules to Springfield and fetch Dr. Kenneth Kirk. A baby was about to be born. My mother told me later that I weighed in at more than 10 pounds. The family nicknamed me Buddy; my brothers often ragged on me how they almost froze their butts off going for the doctor.

My first memories of the home at the mill were the activities that took place there, primarily in the kitchen, the center of all home activities. I remember lying in the window surrounded by geraniums, enjoying the morning sun streaming in, and warming me, after I had been breast-fed by Mom. I could look out and see the rock fence that my dad built, then beyond to a green cottage where Rollie Lambert lived. Booley Evans and his wife Sally lived and operated a store in the old mill that was mostly a beer joint.

From a window at my home I watched my dad and the neighbors build an icehouse. Dad filled it with ice that he cut from the river and drug the ice by mule team to the icehouse. He covered the ice with layers of sawdust to keep it from melting. The ice was sold to campers in the cottages during the summer and Booley bought ice from dad to keep the beer cold at his bar.

Many times I would awaken on a blanket next to the sewing machine. I loved to watch my mom operate the treadle with her foot. A large wheel spun and it had a belt that went up to the head where Mom guided material under the needle as she made dresses and shirts for us kids. The name "Singer" was cast into the framework that held the treadle and wheel. Once I remember fooling around the wheel and getting my finger stuck between the belt and the wheel, ripping the skin from my finger. Mom said, "Let that be a lesson to keep your fingers out of places they don't belong."

Me at 18 months outside my
birthplace near Millison's Mill

After my noon feeding, Mom would place me in the window that caught the afternoon sun, and there I could see the chicken coop where the water from the race ran through one corner of the fence. Beyond was the garden with a fence around all four sides on which red roses climbed. Sometimes Grannie, our cow, would be allowed to graze in the yard and often Mom would yell at Grannie when the gentle bovine pooped in the path to the kitchen door. Mom would say, "In all my born days I'll never understand why she poops in the path when she could go elsewhere." Often when I awoke from my afternoon naps, I needed changing in the worst way, and Mom would give me a nice bath and turn me loose on the linoleum floor. My world was wonderful and it seemed that it would never end.

Once I was weaned from being breast-fed, Mom began putting me in bed with Dad and my brother Jesse. My sisters Lena, Betty and Georgia all slept upstairs in one bed. Mom mostly slept on the couch. When Clyde, Tuck and Bill came home, they had to sleep on the floor. My dad had this game he would play in bed with Jesse and me. It was called "spoon." We would all face the wall and at the command of "spoon," all three of us would turn at the same time and end up in the other direction. We fit on the bed better as "spoons."

I spent a lot of time on the front porch with Buckeye, our dog, who was black and white and had beautiful long hair. We were inseparable and I loved him. He would dig to China if I said, "Dig, boy!" Mom told me not to go beyond the little bridge over the race so Buckeye and I would lie on the footbridge and I would strain to reach as far down as I could to catch tadpoles and minnows. One day, I fell into the race and my head was buried in the mud. Buckeye barked and my sister Betty rescued me. She and Mom pounded on my back until I puked and coughed mud from my windpipe. I learned to blow my nose, and mud came out for days.

My brother Tuck loved to fish and hunt. I remember him trapping muskrats along the river, skinning them and stretching their pelts over boards he had shaped. He had box traps into which he caught rabbits that supplied the family with rabbit meat. On occasion he would come home smelling real bad; he would have caught a skunk in one of his traps. He wouldn't turn it loose for its pelt was worth money. My brother Jesse often went hunting with Tuck, and when Tuck worked shifts at the B & O Railroad, Jesse tended the traps. I couldn't wait to be big enough to do the traps.

I learned that I could remain on the house side of the footbridge and make it to see Sally Evans at the mill and not have to cross the race. I thought it would be nice to take a gift to Sally. I was able to reach the hen's nests, and decided a couple of eggs would be a nice gift. I knew she had a big jar of gingersnap cookies on the bar and maybe if I were not too forward, she would take the hint, and give me some gingersnaps without my asking. Mom did not allow me to beg for anything. Sally liked the exchange of eggs for gingersnaps, and almost every day I'd visit the hen house and get the eggs. If there weren't any eggs in the nest I'd practically have my hand under the hen waiting for the egg to drop. The hens pecked my hands when I'd reach under them, but the pain was not too big of a price for a handful of gingersnaps.

There was a rain barrel just outside Sally's back porch in which Booley kept snap'n turtles. He would fatten them up and Sally would make turtle soup. One day, I lifted the wooden lid on the rain barrel and took a peek. A big ole' turtle hissed and drew his head into his shell.

Sometimes I left the mill and stopped at Rolly Lambert's. He lived in a little green cottage between our house and the mill and I knew that he also had a stash of gingersnap cookies. But he was a little stingy, only giving me two snaps when I visited him. I think he wanted in on the egg deal, but I never offered.

One day, I had some warm, just-laid eggs in my front pockets and was on my way to Sally's. I stubbed my toe on something and fell down and busted both eggs. I had egg mess running down my legs onto my bare feet and even on my private parts. When I got to Sally's the only thing I could think of doing was cry, and it worked. She gave me a bunch of cookies and she got a wash pan full of warm water and a towel, and told me to take my britches off. Well, I wasn't going to let her see my private parts so I turned away, dropped my britches, and wrapped myself in the towel. Sally started bathing me with the washcloth and washed my feet and when she got near the "impossible area," she handed me the washcloth. Sally then washed out my britches and draped them on the porch railing to dry.

She had a big pot boiling on her stove and I could hear a lot of thrashing around in the pot so I asked her, "What are you cooking?"

She said, "Turtle."

"Do you cook turtle alive?" I inquired.

She said, "No, but turtle meat pops and jerks about in the pot when it cooks."

"I don't believe you, please let me see."

Sally pulled up a chair and allowed me to get near the pot. She lifted the lid and sure enough, the meat was jerking around and twitching about like it was still alive. Suddenly, I was splashed with scalding broth. Sally put some butter on a spot on my arm where I was burnt.

Mom appeared on Sally's back porch and said she was worried about where her Buddy was. Mom would come to see Sally at the back of the store and in her kitchen, but she would never be caught dead or alive coming in the front door of the store, for it was a "beer joint"—Mom hated alcohol of any kind. Mom asked why my britches were wet. Sally told the whole story. Mom gave me a warning that if I stole any more eggs she would tan my "siplus." The wrong words to describe "butt" could get you in trouble with Mom, for she knew the words that God liked and everyone had better not use a word that God didn't like around her or you would pay the consequences.

During the summer months, the Burton sisters, Kitty, Maude and Jesse, came to one of the cottages along the river. The cottage had a lot of steps leading down to the river and a small boat dock. My family had known these schoolteachers for some time.

One day the Burton sisters brought me to their cottage and gave me a gift; it was a cork gun. This was the first time I had ever seen a girl in a bathing suit. I didn't have a bathing suit; when I went in the water I swam in my clothes or buck naked. Their suits were one piece and their white legs reminded me of two long pieces of chalk sticking out; it was the first time I had ever noticed a woman's legs that far up. They teased me to get me to talk and tell them stories. They made some vegetable soup and offered me a bowl, and after I had finished it they asked me how I liked it. I said, "It would be okay, but you should cabbage it up a little to be good soup like Mom's." I think the girls caught me looking at them; I wondered whether they could ever have babies, for the baby would starve to death because they were flat as a pancake on top.

The sisters walked me home and Buckeye followed along through the cornfield and by our barn where our two mules, Beck and Belle, lived. The hog pen smelled awful as we passed it and the girls acted like they had never smelled anything that bad, but I knew better. Their outhouse at the cottage smelled worse.

I loved my new cork gun and each time I would shoot it, Buckeye would go to the cork and wait for me to pick it up. I don't know what got into my head but one sunny day, I decided that since I had a gun, the time was right, for me to go hunting. Buckeye loved walking along the river and he sniffed and dug at each hole he came to. I stood there with my gun cocked and ready to fire. Nothing ever came out of the holes. The riverbank was slippery and every now and then I would slide down the bank toward the river. I had heard my dad and brothers talking about "a terrible whirlpool" that was formed in the river at the place where the water from the spring-fed crick dumped into the river. They said the whirlpool could suck you down under the water, and even if you could swim, you would be a goner if you fell in the river at that place. When I saw a swirl in the river and some leaves being sucked under, that was enough for me. I began to hightail it home, but I became so tired and sleepy that I laid down where an old millstone had been discarded.

Mom missed me after lunch and by the time she was able to get my sisters, the campers and other people out looking for me it was nearly dark. They saw where I had slipped down toward the river and Mom was crying and screaming that her baby was gone! My sister Georgia found Buckeye and me. I thought I would get my siplus beat off, but Mom just held me and gave me my supper and put me to bed. As she sat by the bed and prayed over me, the kerosene lamp cast her shadow on the wall. I heard her words but didn't understand what a "soul" was; she wanted mine to be kept by God. I repeated after her:

> "Now I lay me down to sleep,
> I pray the Lord my soul to keep,
> If I should die before I awake,
> I pray the Lord my soul to take.
>   Amen."

My life was becoming more complicated; I had begun to think about more things than watching out for snakes, spiders, wood ticks and the like. Now, I was thinking about things such as secrets and praying. And on a daily basis when I tried to sleep my mind was on all kind of stuff, like learning the right words to speak at the proper time; the words that Mom liked and the words that God liked and such. Sometimes, I heard words at the barn, "barn language," and words at Booley's barroom, "barroom language;" my concern was that I couldn't use either of these languages in Mom's kitchen.

Dad had talked to Mr. Callahan about farming some land on the other side of the river. He told Mom he would be able to ford the river at the rapids with the mules and take the plow over in the boat and if he needed other farm equipment, Mr. Callahan had almost every tool required. To my absolute surprise, Dad told Mom that he was taking me with him across the river. Wow! I was going with Dad to the field! We walked down to the edge of the river to where he had a wooden boat tied up. We got in the boat and Dad rowed across to the other side. As we walked along a narrow cowpath through the grassy field, I had to scramble through the high grass to be able to stay alongside. I definitely wanted to stay with Dad and not lag behind. As Dad stopped to survey the field, I was standing on a high spot in the grass—but the ground moved! I jumped up and grabbed my dad around his mid-section and yelled at the turtle I was standing on, "You old son of a b—h, what are you doing sneaking around in the grass?" I just knew that Dad was going to skin me alive for using such "field language," but I could feel his chest sort of pulsing in and out and he was looking away. I wasn't sure whether he was getting ready to unload on me or just chuckling, but it turned out that he was chuckling and I didn't say another word about the turtle. We finished the trip to the Callahan fields and returned back across the river and Dad tied up the boat. Dad didn't say anything to Mom about my using "field language" when he talked about the trip. I was so proud that Dad took me to the field. We also shared a common secret about that turtle and that I was bilingual.

My sister, Lena, invited a friend, Dorothy Harris, home to spend the weekend. My sisters Lena, Betty and Georgia took Dorothy and me to the river to swim. I had to sit on the bank of the river for I couldn't swim and the water was deep at the place we called "the rock." When Dorothy and Lena were trying to swim from the rock ledge at the bank of the river to "the rock" in the middle of the river Dorothy tired and was unable to continue. She grabbed Lena, who was not a strong swimmer. Betty and Georgia saw what was happening and dove into the water and saved both of them from drowning. Lena never went swimming again after that.

When the girls talked about the incident to Mom they said that Dorothy just didn't have any strength to swim the distance. Mom didn't have the answer for the question why Dorothy couldn't swim the distance to the rock. Dorothy was a beautiful girl, very delicate, black hair and dark eyes with long eyelashes.

I noticed that Dad was not working at the tie plant in Green Spring; I overheard Mom telling a neighbor that he had hurt his back very bad. The accident occurred after he and uncle Clarence decided they could make more money loading and unloading ties as a one-man job instead of a two-man job. When a heavy tie got away from Dad, he hurt his back. Uncle Clarence said he was fortunate that he only hurt his back, for the 500-pound tie could have crushed him.

Dad was a good handyman and our neighbors and the campers in the cottages always needed something fixed. He also had a roadside stand where he sold his vegetables and melons during the summer. During the fall, winter and spring he worked for the WPA on road projects near home, but it wasn't steady work and we had to rely on the farm's cash crops.

When Dad did handyman work he was paid in various ways: a couple of chickens, a pig, a load of hay, or sometimes cash. He often used the cash to buy beer at the Mill. Mom hated that he was spending a lot of time there and coming home "two sheets to the wind." I could overhear them fussing about Dad's drinking. One evening my three older brothers, all in their early 20s, confronted Dad about his drinking and in return, he got on to them about their appearing at mealtimes and never working around the place anymore. A scuffle broke out in the kitchen and Dad threw the three of them out of the house. They didn't spend much time around home after that; however, Mom always invited them for meals.

More and more campers were coming to the river, and they seemed to have nice cars and more money to spend at the roadside stand and at the Mill. Times seemed to be getting better. Sometimes, the campers would take me for a ride in their cars; two grownups would jump in the rumble seat and someone would toss me in between. Life was great and it seemed everyone was happier than before.

2

The river floods

We were having a lot of rain, and our neighbors were talking about the river over-flowing its banks and possibly flooding the Millsons Mill area.

I had just turned five years old.

After a couple more days of heavy rain, the crick and river continued to swell and the river was over its banks at the Bend. I could hear grownups talking about cloudbursts upstream and more rain on the way. Dad was good at predicting the weather, and he thought that the rain would soon quit. The rain continued and everyone was talking about how the river was leaving its bank at the Callahan farm across the river from our place and at various other places. The cricks and runs were flooding the roads, and there were major washouts in many places.

Our chickens hated the rain. They were in the coop because the race had swollen so much that they couldn't get out into their yard. The water was only a few inches below the bottom of the footbridge that crossed the race. My brother Tuck came by and said that the roads were bad from Springfield and that it was too late now to gather his traps from along the river; he would have to hope that the trap chains would hold or he would lose his traps. Neighbors were making plans for someone to stand watch during the night. The rain continued to fall.

I slept pretty well and none of my family seemed too concerned, for we had high water almost every spring during the snowmelt and runoff, and on our side of the river, the Millsons Mill side, there was a high protective bank. I could hear people talk about bringing their boats to high ground. They said the dock at the Burtons' cottage was under water and some of the steps were covered. Dad came to the house and announced that he was loading the wagon with stuff from the barn because it appeared to him that the river was going to break over the bank on our side.

The mules hated rain, almost as much as the chickens did, and they had their ears turned backward and down as they sloshed through the mud, pulling the wagon. The wheels were cutting deep into the water-soaked ground. I watched

Dad opened the upper gate to the cow pasture where Grannie was grazing with her new calf. He decided he was going to tie the mules and Grannie to trees and leave them out all night on high ground. He talked to Mom about turning the pigs out because they were too heavy to lift onto the wagon and he didn't have hog crates to haul them to higher ground. They discussed whether pigs could swim and Dad said that they could and do a good job at it, but if they were fat their front hooves would often cut their throats and that's what would do them in. They decided to leave the pigs in their pen until the water was so high the animals wouldn't want to break back to their pens. Mom and Dad knew that when hogs were set loose they became unpredictable and when they were scared they generally would go back to their pens first. Mom tried to chase the chickens away from the coop, but they would get on the chickenhouse roof and sit there. She was hoping they would go to the woods and roost in the trees next to the mules.

I could see the river from the second floor of our house. Large things like stumps, dead trees, and barrels were floating down. Someone told Mom that the Burtons' dock and steps were gone. The water was in the cornfield by the barn and was running between the barn and the cottages along the edge of the river. Dad turned the hogs loose and, as he figured, they began running around their pen looking for a way in. He tried and tried to herd them to dry ground. They wouldn't budge.

Soon the water was solid from the riverbank to the road in front of our house. The Woodson family was forced to leave their home because it had water running through the back door and out the front. It wasn't long before the Burton cottage floated away, followed by all the cottages along the riverbank. Watching the current you could see sheds, cottages, barns, and animals floating downstream. When the buildings and sheds hit each other they would turn and twist and heave up and down and the roofs would explode off the buildings due to the air pressure built up inside. The beautiful sycamore trees were starting to lean and before long some were uprooted and swept away. The river was full of stuff.

Dad came into the house and yelled, "The house isn't safe. We've got to leave now!" He began giving instructions and everyone frantically moved furniture to the upper level. We all grabbed clothing, mattresses, and pillows and carried them to a cottage up on the ridge where we would spend the night—the last and only cottage on high ground.

My brothers, Jesse and Tuck, were using a boat to help people get their belongings to higher ground; they were able to row across the flooded fields. Mom told my sister Betty that she was to take care of me, and Betty put me on her shoulders. We looked like drowned rats with mud all over our clothes. My sisters were wearing cotton dresses that stuck to their bodies and their hair was soaked, but none of us complained. For the first time, I saw hopelessness in my mom's face as she got into the boat at the back steps of our house and the boat moved away from the porch. I heard Mom praying for God to stop the rain and for the floodwaters to go away.

Just about all the neighbors around Millisons Mill were at the cottage. Their mattresses were piled high on the cottage floor.

It was starting to get dark. The river had larger objects floating in it, including cottages, animals, just about anything you could imagine. We could see that water was up to the first floor windows of our home and a curtain was floating in the muddy water that flowed out the window. Then, as we were watching, a window blew out. Tuck said it was the air pressure that built up as the water rose in the house. The chicken coop floated away with the chickens riding on the roof. We never saw them again.

Sally had brought some food from the store and opened cans of pork and beans. It was my first time eating from tin cans. Mom kept telling us to hold back for it wasn't our food. Frankly, the beans tasted strange anyhow; they needed a big hunk of pork to season them.

I heard Mom yelling, "Where's John Russell?" That's what she called my dad. Everyone began looking around the cottage but he wasn't at the cottage. Jesse and Tuck came rowing the boat to the cottage steps and yelled, "Dad and Booley are still in the Mill drinking beer and we can't get them to come to the cottage." Mom said to Jesse and Tuck, "Take Buddy down there in the boat to get them. John Russell will come home if Buddy asks him." My brothers rowed the boat toward the Mill, being careful not to get in the swift current of the main river. When I got out of the boat and stepped onto the front porch of the Mill, the water was squirting up through the cracks on the floorboards. My brothers yelled, "Get in there and tell Dad to come out. This place is about to float away!" The Mill was dark inside but I could see Booley and Dad sitting at the bar. Water was about two inches deep in the place. I asked Dad to come with me because I couldn't sleep in the cottage without him, and the women were crying and praying and all their fuss scared me. He and Booley came out on the porch and we got Dad in the boat. Booley was a large man and he had to wait for the next trip.

People became concerned that the cottage might not be a safe place and they began marking the steps to determine how fast the water was rising. We couldn't sleep. Many people prayed all night. Sometime during the blackness the rain quit and the water rose almost to the last step on the front porch of the cottage; that was the high-water mark.

The next day the sun was shining. We could look down and see the devastation: our home had water running out the upstairs windows and our barn was gone, Rolly Lambert's cottage was covered, the Mill had water running through the top of the first-floor windows. Three cottages were stuck against trees at the crick near the Woodson house. The cottages were on their sides and all catawampus. Everything imaginable was in the trees and along the high-water edge. We could see many dead animals hanging from the trees and stuck against the buildings.

It was three days before anyone could enter our home, and then Dad reported that we would not be able to return, for the place was full of mud. He told Mom that he would remove what was left from the upstairs rooms, and told all of us that we would have to find another place to live.

3

Starting over

We moved to the Hedrick house, a place that the Washington family, our black neighbors at the bend, had abandoned. The house was about a half mile from the mill. It was a flimsily built house and had no barn or outbuildings; you could see daylight through the cracks in the sideboards, which had never been painted. Mom had to put buckets around to catch the water dripping from leaks in the roof when it rained. If you laid a marble down on the floor it would roll to the wall. We had room in the attic for only two beds. The house did have a porch around two sides, the roof leaked there also. The few pieces of furniture we had salvaged were coming apart as they dried out, and everything we brought from home at the mill smelled like river mud. We had to carry water from a spring about a quarter of a mile from the house, along a path that edged along a rock ledge above the crick, the same crick that fed the water to the race in front of our home at the mill.

The first thing Dad did was to build a bridge across the crick so we didn't have to jump from stone to stone to get from the road to the house. Next, he built a shelter for Beck and Belle, our mules, and Grannie the cow. We didn't have fences so the animals were tied out until fences were up. The pigs and chickens never came back. The flood destroyed almost all of the food that we had canned and stored at the old house. Mom was sad that she lost her potted flowers and also that she didn't have curtains for the windows. We all felt naked and cold at the new place.

Our family was in a bad way; we had no money and little food. The girls and Jesse went back to school at Springfield. Aunt Ella, Mom's sister, who lived over an old gas station in Springfield, provided them lunch because there wasn't any food at home to send with them. Friends and neighbors were helping us; my mom and dad didn't want to accept help but people helped us anyhow and the family appreciated it.

Mom took in washing from Mr. Campbell, one of our new neighbors. She carried water from the spring and heated it outdoors in two black iron pots. Using a scrub board in a #10 washtub, Mom washed the clothes. She used a blanket to pad the kitchen table and heated flat irons on the kitchen stove to iron the clothes. It was difficult for me to keep up with all the things that Mom was doing, for she always had about five things going at once: baking bread or a cake, cooking the next meal, feeding the chickens, milking Grannie, butchering a chicken. Sometimes neighbor women would send for her to be with them when they were ready to have a baby, and often she would remain with them all night. Mom delivered many babies and the people she helped would bring by chickens or other items such as a mess of greens or other vegetables that they had grown, or sometimes clothing that they had made.

Before long winter was upon us. We almost froze in the Hedrick house; our wood stove just could not heat the place. Dad's work at the WPA was spotty because with the ground frozen, the men often were sent home. The family gathered walnuts, hazelnuts and hickory nuts. We had a family of flying squirrels that lived in the attic of the house and we had to take special measures to keep them from stealing our nuts. Dad, Tuck and Jesse hunted squirrels, rabbits, turkeys and deer to keep meat on the table. Tuck and Jesse were both good fishermen but after the flood the only kind they caught were catfish and eels.

The field along the crick, which Dad could plow for a garden, did not have rich soil like the river-bottom fields he farmed at the mill; he had to deal with rocks and patches of nearly useless soil. He was able to sharecrop a piece of land directly across the crick from the house. The soil there was good and he plowed it to plant corn for the animals. He also farmed a patch against the side of the mountain far from the house; he would load the wagon with the plow and other implements and drive the team for over an hour to get to that field. It was so steep that he had to use a special hillside plow to till the rocky ground. Dad believed it would be good for buckwheat. It was so far away that Mom and he worked out a system of signals using sheets hung on the clothesline in configurations that indicated when supper would be ready and Dad could figure when to leave the field and be home on time for supper.

The Blue family lived up the crick from us. The mother's name was Mammie and one of the daughters, Martha Ann, was my age. I was bashful, so it took me a long while to gain enough courage to talk to her. Going to visit Mammie was like medicine for Mom; aside from talking to the family she seldom had anyone to share conversation.

On one of the visits, Mom and Mammie were in the house and Martha Ann and I were in the back yard playing. Martha Ann loved to play ring around the rosy. I didn't care for it but went along. She also enjoyed playing house and she tried to get me to eat mud pie, but I wouldn't. She had a few tin cans that she said had various foods in them. I couldn't understand all the make-believe stuff she was doing. She chattered and chattered like a magpie, it seemed without end, and I couldn't get a word in edgewise. That particular day she had one of those round Quaker Oats boxes. She had removed the lid and removed the bottom and it became a wide tube. I don't recall which one of us came up with the idea, but we decided it would be fun to see if we could pee through the tube without hitting the sides. About that time Mom and Mammie came around the house and screamed, "What are you doing?" Mom grabbed me by the ear and told me to go straight home and wait for her. I wasn't sure what the fuss was about but I knew it had to do with our plans with the oatmeal box. Darned if things weren't getting too complicated for me with a girl in my life.

As I walked along the sandy path to the house, I noted a colony of doodlebug traps. I got down flat on my belly beside the traps and began to repeat, "Doodle, doodle, doodle." I could see grains of sand sliding down the conical sides of the trap and the little critter at the bottom getting excited and moving into position to catch an ant that might slid into its trap. Dad had earlier tried to get me to believe that the doodlebug could hear and understand my voice, but I had already figured it out that it was the breeze from my breath that caused the grains of sand to slide down the walls of the trap and that's what got the doodle bug (ant lion) excited.

Mom didn't whip me for the oatmeal box caper but she ignored me. I knew our relationship was strained and that she didn't want to address the subject of my behavior around a girl.

My brother Clyde met Hazel Wertz in Centerville, Pennsylvania, and they married in June 1937. Soon thereafter, my sister Lena married a young man by the name of Robert Lee Fuller, a mechanic at the Chevy garage in Romney. When Lena and Robert Lee left on their honeymoon, Lena wanted to kiss me goodbye but I ran to the back of the house and crawled under the porch. Betty soon joined me; she said she wanted to have a good cry. In our family crying in public was about the worst and most shameful thing you could do and my family seldom kissed.

Tuck dated and married Dorothy Harris and they moved into the house across the crick from where we lived. This was good because we all liked Dorothy a lot and she seemed to appreciate anything we did for her. My brother, Bill, was dating a girl in the Bedford Valley and Mom believed it wouldn't be long until they married.

With family members leaving, I thought I needed to do more things to help around the house. I was able to carry a couple of gallon-size syrup tins filled with water from the spring. Mom was so proud of me, even when I spilled most of the water trying to walk the toe path and not fall into the crick. She told me what a great job I was doing.

One of Mom's set'n hens had a bunch of peeps and they were running around the woodpile area. I don't understand what got into me, but I decided I would do like Mom, and use the axe to chop off the heads of a few chickens, just to help her out. I put a peep on the chopping block and cut it in half and then I did another one. Mom saw me using the axe and came over to see what I was doing. She was really upset at me, for killing her baby peeps. She had me dig two graves and bury the little bodies. She wanted me to say a prayer for them, their mommy and their little brothers and sisters. I had no idea what to say, so I recited, "I lay these peeps down to sleep and pray the Lord their souls to keep, Amen."

My sister Betty went to live with Lena and Robert Lee in order that she could attend high school in Romney. Clyde and Hazel had a son, Eugene. Mom was proud of being a grandmother.

Although our family had shrunk from ten to five at home, because we only had two beds in the house I continued to sleep with Dad and Jesse. One winter night it snowed and the wind blew very hard and we had white lines across our bed from where the snow came through the cracks. On cold nights we would jump into bed wearing our long underwear and Dad would have us cover our heads so that our breath would heat under the covers. Mom heated bricks for Georgia and her to warm their feet and bed. Mom wouldn't let Dad bank the heating stove to last the night. She was afraid to sleep with the fire burning because she remembered her first house burning to the ground when a downdraft was created which blew hot coals from the fireplace into the living room. It was a cabin at a logging camp near Kitzmiller, Maryland.

Buckeye was missing. He didn't come home for days. Dad finally found him and it appeared that a snake had bitten him for his body was swollen. I wasn't allowed to go see our dog. Dad and Jesse buried Buckeye. A few days later, Dad came home with a new puppy that we called "Rover." He was reddish colored, a shorthaired pooch that followed Dad everywhere. Dad didn't like that; he wanted the dog to stay with us kids and be a watchdog at the house. After being scolded many times Rover finally got the message and stayed around home most of the time.

A family by the name of Haines moved into our old house at the mill. Mr. Haines told Dad it took them almost a year to get the mud out of the house and fix it to be livable. The Haines had a son, Kenneth, who was a few years older than me. He had a bicycle and his father allowed him to ride it to Cherry's store in Springfield. One day I was near the steep hill on the road to Springfield and saw Kenneth going very fast down the hill. He missed the curve at the bottom and plunged off the road into a briar thicket. I ran through the crick and across the stile over the Blues' fence, and when I got to the thicket, I could hear him groaning. The thorns had cut almost every inch of his body, yet he could walk. After we got the bike out I asked him what happened. He said he bought some bubble gum at Cherry's and blew a big bubble that burst over his eyes, so he let go of the handlebar to get the gum off and ran off the road. We stopped by the house and Mom fixed him up. When she put some iodine on his cuts he screamed real loud. He told Mom that he healed real easy and he didn't need any additional medical attention.

4

School at last

I had a new pair of shoes for school, and a new pair of britches. Mom insisted that I wear underwear to school. She bought some summer underwear through a catalogue. Everything fit pretty well except that the shoes gave me blisters, but I never complained to anyone. We had to pay for our own books at school; I was able to use hand-me-down spelling and primer books. Mom got me a pencil and a nice writing tablet that was thicker than the one she used for writing letters. My tablet was red and it had an Indian chief on the cover.

The Springfield school was a square, wooden two-story building painted white. A set of open stairs on the outside was used only as a fire escape by the fifth-through eighth-graders. Upstairs, Miss Browning taught the fifth and sixth grades and Mr. Loy taught the seventh and eighth grades and was the principal. Downstairs, Mr. Reynolds taught the third and fourth grade and Mrs. Barnes, my teacher, taught first and second grade.

Mrs. Barnes was nice, sort of short and plump, and she did something that I hated. She would grab me and pull me to her big bosom that smelled like a lilac bush and squeeze so hard I had to clinch my "siplus" to keep from breaking wind.

We didn't have books at home but the schoolroom had some books and magazines. When Mrs. Barnes said we needed 50 cents to pay for one year of *The Weekly Reader* I had a terrible time asking Mom and Dad, because I knew money was tight in our family. Somehow they scratched it up and soon I was bringing a magazine into our home each week. We all read it many times.

One day the school had a person who was looking for lice. She lined us up and checked our heads and some of the kids got dusted. When it was over the woman asked if we had seen any of our family members scratching their heads. I raised my hand and told them that my brother Jesse, in the seventh grade scratched his head a lot. The lice checker went directly to Jesse's room, got him out of class and checked his head. Jesse waited until supper to tell Mom and Dad that I had told the school people that our family had lice. This turned out to be worse than any-

thing I had ever done in all my born days—I had shamed our family in public!
Having lice was very shameful and Mom and Dad were sure everyone in Springfield would think we all had them. Everyone in the family shunned me. I went to
bed first that night.

I decided on a way I could get back at my family. Each time anyone scratched
his or her head I would call attention to it until finally they would quit looking at
me like I was really dumb. I also let them know that even though we had bedbugs
in our beds, that they didn't have to worry, I would never tell anyone. Georgia
said, "Oh my Heavens, don't you say a word." I grinned, knowing I was back in
the fold tighter than a tick and said, "I won't tell anyone."

Mom and Dad had a rule that each day that I was good at school I would
receive a penny and if I was bad I would lose a penny, and a spanking was a
month's worth of losing pennies. So I made really sure that I never had a losing
month. I did very well in the first grade, all passing marks, zero times tardy. I
even received a certificate signed by the big shots at the school for perfect attendance.

Money continued to become tighter. When our shoes wore out, Dad used a
shoe last to fashion soles from some pieces of rubber and leather he had stored
away. Our school lunches were generally a piece of homemade bread with jam on
it.

One day I overheard Dad telling Mom that we couldn't make ends meet at
this place and he was going to go look for a different place to sharecrop or find an
hourly job.

Second grade was going real well. I was in the bluebird reading group and we
bluebirds knew we were good because we were reading from a third grade-reader,
a blue book. The rest of the class was reading from a red book, a second grade
book. I liked to tease other kids, especially the girls. Some liked it and some
didn't. Stella, a small, skinny girl, hated it but also seemed to love it. She
delighted in bumping me when she passed my desk. She had knobby knees and
straight, blonde hair that she flipped around, and she would cock her nose in the
air and make like she never bumped me.

Me in second grade at Springfield school

It was just before Easter and I was at the bluebird table, cutting a piece of lace paper to glue onto a beautiful red Easter card for Mom. Stella had sharpened her pencil at the sharpener mounted on the windowsill. I was standing and working at the table, and I was expecting Stella to bump me. When she got near me she bumped me and said, "Give me those clizzers!"

I said, "What?"

She got right up in my face and yelled, "Give me those clizzers!"

"No." I snapped back and said, "If you can't say scissors, then you don't get them."

Thud. She jabbed the sharpened pencil into my right side. Without thinking, I hit her—*BAM*—on the chin. She went down on the floor and the kids started screaming. Mrs. Barnes came running toward me with a paddle so I ran to the back of the room to go out the back door but I couldn't open it. Then I figured I could get under the desk at the back of the row and crawl to the front of the room under the desks so she couldn't hit me as I crawled forward. Then I could scoot out the front door. But when I ducked under the first seat I hit the footboard and I was trapped there with my "siplus" sticking up. Mrs. Barnes started pounding with the paddle while she was telling someone to pick Stella up and put a wet towel on her head. She kept hitting me until her strength gave out. Then she got hold of my right ear and started dragging me upstairs to the principal's office. She told Mr. Loy what a terrible thing I had done and said she didn't want me back in her room. Mr. Loy went to his desk and pulled out a rubber hose that was split back to where it formed a handle that was wrapped with white tape. He didn't say a word. He beat me real hard. I didn't cry, so he just kept on, his face becoming bright red. Somehow, I was numb to the pain and I just stood there waiting while Mr. Loy wrote a note to Mom and Dad that said I couldn't come back to school unless they brought me back and reported to him. Then he told me to go home.

As I started walking across the schoolyard I was sure everyone in Springfield would know about this. I thought about going to Aunt Ella's; she lived nearby, not too far from Cherry's store. Instead, I crossed the macadam highway and started walking. I felt like everyone was looking at me. I kicked a lot of gravel as I ambled the two miles home. At the bottom of the big hill across from the Woodson's barn, I could see home and I hated to "face the music," so I stopped and sat under a tree. I saw Dad plowing the field next to Tuck and Dorothy's house. Dorothy was on the porch rocking Herbie, her son and Mom's second grandson.

Despite the punishment I had received, I knew worse was coming. Running away crossed my mind. I didn't want to go home and I couldn't go back to the schoolroom. It was time for a good cry so I sat there under the tree and did just that. My tears stopped when a red squirrel started chattering at me and wouldn't shut up.

Dorothy had gone inside, so I didn't have to face her as I passed her house. When I got to the sycamore tree where the footbridge crossed the crick I thought again about scooting off, but Mom came onto the porch of our house, saw me and said, "Plumb my soul to goodness. What is wrong? Why aren't you in school?"

I showed her the note. She held her hand to her mouth, made a sharp gasp, and then said, "Take the note to your Dad."

The footbridge seemed twice as long as I re-crossed it and began walking through the plowed field to where Dad was plowing. Birds were eating worms and grubs from the freshly turned earth. I could smell the soil. Beck and Belle were hitched to the plow, they were wet with sweat; white froth from the sweat outlined their harness and collar. They twisted their heads to peer around their blinders to look at me. Dad said, "Whoa." The team stopped. Dad also was soaked with sweat, his face streaked with dirt and his hands covered with a grimy mixture of sweat and soil. He looked at me and said, "What are you doing home from school?"

I showed him the note and he said, "I don't have my glasses, tell me what happened."

"My teacher had to beat me for hitting a girl," I replied.

A big frown spread across his face and he asked, "You hit a girl?"

"Yes," I answered and right then I knew I was in big trouble. Dad had always instructed us boys to never hit a girl. Then I told him how the principal had beaten me and sent me home with the note.

"You got two beat'ns at school?" he asked. Then he tied off the reins that encircled his waist and walked toward Beck to unbuckle a harness strap from her collar. He said, "Come here and bend over."

I bent over his knee and he gave me a real good whipping. My yelling was so loud the birds began to fly out of the field. Beck and Belle became rigid and their bodies shook when they heard the leather hitting flesh. "Go to the house," Dad said.

I had run out of tears. My chest was heavy for causing Dad and Mom so much pain. I again crossed the footbridge, walked onto the porch and laid the note on the Victrola as I went upstairs to bed. This was the worst day in all my born days.

I could smell supper but no one called for me. I heard Dad tell Mom that he wasn't going to that damned school to talk to the principal because we would be moving on the first of April. Mom raised her voice as she asked, "What's going on?"

Dad said, "Mr. Callahan knows a businessman from Cumberland, Maryland, by the name of Mr. Randolph Millholland, who had a place in Spring Gap, Maryland. He needs a sharecropper to farm his place and tend his orchards. Mr. Millholland would be able to get a government farm loan that wouldn't have to be repaid until there was a crop that made a profit."

Early the next morning, Mom informed me that she would be riding the bus to school and would go to the principal's office with me. I about died. This thing is going too far, I thought.

When Mom got on the bus all the kids were looking at me and I felt ashamed. When we reached Mr. Loy's office he told me to sit in the hall while he talked with Mom. After a time they came out to inform me that I would apologize to Stella Mason in front of the class, with Mom, Mr. Loy and Mrs. Barnes looking on.

I wasn't sure what apologize meant or how I would do it but Mom cleared that up when she said, "You tell Stella that you're sorry for hitting her and will never do it again."

Protesting, I showed Mom the pencil lead imbedded under my skin. But she said, "Don't talk about that. We will have to do what the principal and I agreed to do."

I said, "Okay, I'll apologize."

All the kids froze when Mr. Loy opened Mrs. Barnes' door. He announced, "Kenneth Shipe has something to say to Stella Mason and the class," and he asked Stella to stand.

I went over to her. My eyes focused on a little rose sewn onto the left collar of her dress. I could tell she was as scared as I was. Her chin was pink from where I had hit her. I stared at the rose and said in my trembling voice, "I am very sorry for hitting you. Please forgive me."

Stella nodded, her head going up and down and her blond hair flopping as she nodded, but she didn't say a word. Mr. Loy said, "Kenneth, apologize to the class and Mrs. Barnes."

I hesitated because that wasn't in the deal. I looked at Mom and she motioned for me to do it. So I looked straight toward the back of the room, keeping my eyes focused on the ABC chart on the wall above the blackboard as I said, "I am sorry for being bad. Please forgive me." The kids, all sitting at attention, didn't show any reaction.

After Mr. Loy and Mom left the room, Mrs. Barnes told everyone to move up one seat so as to fill my vacant seat, and instructed me to sit in the back row near where Henry sat. He was a big kid about 11 years old who had repeated second grade since he was eight and he hardly ever attended class.

None of the kids talked to me much after the big problem I caused, but it didn't make any difference to me for I knew a secret—in three weeks, Kenneth Shipe was moving to Maryland and I didn't care how these kids treated me for I'd soon have a bunch of new pals. I didn't like this school anymore.

5

Higher ground on Martins Mountain

It was April Fools' Day 1940, and Dad and Mr. Haines struggled to load Mom's kitchen stove on the back of the borrowed truck and install the tail gate. They were wiping the sweat from their foreheads and talking about how heavy the cook stove was, and Mom was fuss'n at Dad about his not wiping the cow manure from the racks of the truck. Adjustments made, Dad announced it was time to load up and Jesse jumped up on the side of the truck and climbed over the top and found a place for us to sit on a chest. Dad helped me climb over the side and said, "Well, we're headin' out. One thing for sure, we won't be flooded out on top of Martins Mountain."

Mom hugged and kissed Dorothy and Herbie, and I could tell everyone was about to cry. Mom and Georgia got in the truck and Dad started the engine. Dorothy was never a strong lady and she didn't look well to me, I could see that she was being very brave and hiding the fact that she would be alone in a place that had few neighbors and a baby boy to care for.

We had to go up around the Blues' house in order to ford the crick at a shallow spot in the stream. Things were happening too fast for me to gather my thoughts; I hadn't really had a chance to say goodbye—goodbye sycamore trees, goodbye stile over the fence, goodbye cowshed. Mammie Blue was waving from her side porch as we circled her house and we all waved a goodbye to Mammie. Stones picked up by the tires were hitting the bottom of the truck and we made a huge dust cloud as we moved up the road toward Springfield.

We came to a stop in Springfield at the edge of the macadam highway, the road from Cumberland to Romney that curved at this spot in Springfield. The large dust cloud caught up with us and we waited a few minutes for the dust to settle. Dad turned the truck to the right and we continued on a dirt road toward Green Spring. Jesse said it was about 15 miles to Green Spring.

The cool April air blowing on us in the back of the truck gave Jesse and me the urge to pee. We decided that we could go over the side of the truck if one of us watched both ways for cars. I went first and sprayed all over the furniture, spotting and streaking the dust that was on everything. Jesse couldn't wait and he went too, with the same effect on the furniture. We hoped that it would rain a few sprinkles so we would be able to blame the streak spots on the weather.

We passed the Green Spring schoolhouse and I saw that it looked much like the Springfield school except it had a tube slide from the second floor for a fire escape versus the steps from the second floor at Springfield school.

Dad slowed the truck to a crawl and nosed it down to a very low bridge that crossed the North Branch of the Potomac River here at Green Spring. The water was nearly black and smelled terrible because it had a creosote oil slick coming from the tie plant. The bridge had only a four-by-four inch timber for a side railing, and the floor was only about six inches above the water. The boards made a clackity-clackity sound as we drove over them. Jesse said the bridge flooded after hard rains, which meant that people living in Oldtown, Maryland had to drive around to Cumberland and back to Green Spring, a trip of almost 75 miles to work at the tie plant. When we reached the Maryland shore, a man came out of a shack and stopped us and Dad had to pay 25 cents toll to cross the bridge.

The truck groaned up the steep bank from the river and we crossed another bridge and Jesse pointed out the Chesapeake and Ohio Canal lock, which hadn't worked for many years and was in bad shape. Jesse and I talked about how water flowing into the lock from upstream would raise a barge and then the upstream gate would open and a mule team would pull the barge out of the lock and head toward Cumberland. If another barge were waiting to enter the lock, the water would be drained from the lock and when it reached the level of the downstream water the mule team would pull the barge out of the lock and head for Washington, D.C.

Passing through Oldtown, Dad drove very slowly on the smooth, macadam streets. Jesse pointed out the big red brick Consolidated School. He said grades 1 through 12 attend the school so we would be attending the same school.

Dad stopped the truck at a railroad crossing, where a huge engine was puffing smoke and blowing steam as it pulled what looked like 87 railroad cars. I was excited; I had never been close to a train before. I saw that some of the cars had people riding in them and the red caboose had Western Maryland Railroad written on it. Jesse said that on an earlier trip with Dad, when they moved the mules over, that Dad had told him about hobos, who rode the railroad cars from city to city looking for work and food.

We crossed the tracks and turned onto a highway made of concrete that led to Cumberland, a road sign showed that this was Maryland Route 51. The truck rode smoothly and Dad was driving much faster. Jesse said we were probably going 35–45 miles per hour. A car passed us and Jesse said it was a 1939 Hudson Terraplane. Boy was it going fast, out of sight in no time.

We passed a beer joint, the Nine Mile Inn. Jesse said, "It's named Nine Mile because it was half way between Oldtown and Cumberland." The place had several signs for beer: Old German, Pabst Blue Ribbon, and Old Export. We talked about how the roads in West Virginia didn't have as many signs as here.

The truck stopped at a gas station and store, the Millstone, a stone building with two Esso gas pumps out front and groceries and a beer parlor inside. Dad told Jesse to pump the gas. A man came out and introduced himself, "My name is Doc Taschenberger." He said, "My family owns this store and my father, William Taschenberger, lives across the highway and has an active mill there. Welcome to Spring Gap. You'd better make sure the radiator is full of water 'cuz the pull up Martins Mountain is a tough one with the load you've got. A lot of trucks overheat on that two-and-half-mile stretch of steep, mountain road."

Doc said to Dad, "You can start a tab here at the Millstone and any member of the family that you want can charge and you can pay a little each month." He looked at us and said, "You all look like you need something to drink. Why don't you all have a tonic, and Mr. Shipe, you can have an Old German beer."

Dad replied, "Okay, we're thirsty."

Doc looked up at me in the truck and said, "What's your name again? And what would you like?"

I said, "My school name is Kenneth, but you can call me Ken. The family calls me Buddy and I'm not fond of it." I saw a sign for RC Cola and I answered, "I'll have an RC Cola."

Doc went to a case filled with tonic bottles and ice, pulled out an RC, opened it and handed it to me. As I held the bottle high the tonic gushed out into my mouth and ran out my nose and I began to strangle.

Mom yelled, "Hold your arm straight over your head and cough!" I hadn't ever had a drink so strong and I continued to cough and sputter as my family looked at me in disgust while they took their places in the truck.

Passing beside the Millstone store I noted an old worn millstone wheel embedded in the wall. The store had a lot of signs advertising beer, tonic and bread.

The truck, in its very lowest gear, groaned up the dirt road past the edge of a stone quarry and around a sharp left curve that led to a very steep climb. We passed a little, white, wooden church, Mt. Tabor Methodist, on the right that had a graveyard alongside. We could see the dust of a vehicle coming down the mountain and it turned out to be a big truck like the one we were in. The driver pulled way over to the side so that we could pass. We only had about one foot between the trucks when we squeezed by. At one point the road was perched on a rock outcropping and at another place it had an S curve over a ledge of rocks.

We entered a clearing in the woods where an electric line crossed the road. Dad pulled over and stopped. He said, "I want to let the engine cool a little before we drive the rest of the way. We're about half way up the mountain to the house." We were able to look down the sides of the mountain valleys both ways. Jesse said, "This is a beautiful sight."

Dad was stretching his arms and legs when he said, "This view isn't anything. Wait 'til we get to the house. The view is really nice there. And by the way, this is the beginning of the property we will be sharecropping and when we clear this land and plant corn, each row will be over one mile long."

As we continued on, the road was not as steep. We stretched our necks and soon we saw a house with a black metal roof, white sides, and porches in front and back. Another house nearby had a roof that needed repair, and there was a small white cottage near where we turned off the road. Dad backed the truck as close to the house as he could. We all got out and stood there looking at the view. Dad said, "Look, you can see as far as Five Points, West Virginia. And look, there to the right, see the train traveling along the river? That is the Baltimore and Ohio Railroad. The B&O runs along the North Branch of the Potomac River on the West Virginia side."

It wasn't long until Mr. Condy Miller pulled up in a Consolidated Orchard Company truck with a few orchard workers and he said, "Mr. Gilbert Miller, one of the owners, who lives beyond us, had sent us down to help unload your furniture as a neighborly gesture."

I needed to go to the toilet. Dad pointed to the outhouse down the side of the mountain from the house. It had two big seats with one small one between them. It was made with rough lumber from a sawmill, and some of the boards were so warped you could see what was going on outside.

When the furniture was placed in the house and we had our first meal, Dad said, "There is one major difference in living here on Martins Mountain from living in the valley in West Virginia and that is water. Here, every drop of water we use for drinking, bathing, cooking, cleaning and watering the animals will come from one source, rainwater. Here at the house rainwater from the roof is filtered through a sand and charcoal filter and collected into an underground cistern.

Water for the animals is collected from the apple storage shed roof into an open reservoir. We must be careful and not waste any water. The owner of this place, Mr. Millholland, told me that the water collection system should be adequate; however, during drought seasons that might not be true. If we run out of water we will have to haul water from the Reckley Spring on Twiggtown Road which is about a ten-mile round trip. We have a bucket at the pitcher pump here at the house. Be sure that if you prime the pump with water from that bucket to refill the bucket so that the next person that needs to pump water will have water for priming the pump."

Jesse was able to help Dad plow the field in front of the house, with Beck and Belle pulling the plow. After the plowing I was allowed to drive the team to level the field with a spring-tooth harrow and then used a drag to smooth the soil. After one field was prepared Dad started another. After the ground was prepared, furrows were plowed, evenly spaced with straight rows for the seeds. There wasn't any school for a week during Easter and we kept busy preparing for the planting, and settling into our new place.

Mr. Millholland, the owner of our place, came down and he and Dad talked about the farm loan and everything was okay. He wanted Dad to buy a truck so that he could start harvesting the asparagus and haul it to market in Cumberland, and he thought Dad needed another mule. When Dad bought a 1935 red Ford pickup we were excited, because it was the first vehicle that he ever owned.

Me with Beck and Belle behind a harrow. View is east toward Warrior Mountain—1940

The asparagus field was nearly three acres and we had to harvest the asparagus twice a week. It took all of us, crawling along on our hands and knees and using a sharp chisel to cut the asparagus stalks about three inches below the ground. We took care not to break any of the new shoots that were coming up under the ground. After we cut the shoots in the field, we placed the shoots in a three-sided box. When the box was full we cut the bottoms of the shoots off even, placed a gum band around the bunch to hold it together, and placed the bunch in a tub that contained about three inches of water. Often we worked by lantern light and would fill three to four #10 washtubs with asparagus bunches. Dad would rise very early and take the asparagus to the A&P market in Cumberland, which bought all that he could provide, paying 10 cents a bunch. This was the first cash crop we had and Dad was sure we could afford seed and some fertilizer when the asparagus harvest was over.

One afternoon we heard a truck coming and in the back was a mule with his head sticking over the cab, braying as loud as he could. The truck turned into the lane and Dad directed the driver to the barn. Dad said the mule's name was Jack and he was young and a little wild. He put a rope onto Jack's halter and when the tailgate was removed Jack didn't wait for a plank walk to be put in place, he jumped off the truck and began going in a circle, pulling away from Dad as hard as he could. Mom and I went down to see the mule. Jesse and the driver of the truck were there. Dad closed the fence gate and let go of the rope and Jack began to buck with all four feet off the ground and he kicked up his heels. Each time he kicked up his hind legs he would let out a big fart, and us males were laughing out loud and slapping our legs. Mom threw all of us a disgusting look and headed for the house. Dad said, "Jack wouldn't be so gassy after a few days pulling the plow."

With the new mule Jesse could plow with Jack and Beck, using the two larger of the three mules as a team. Dad would put me on Belle's back and use a single-bladed plow to make rows for the crops. The fields were long and narrow, and we could only cultivate the level top part of the mountain. Dad put up a stake and I was to guide Belle toward the stake to keep the rows straight and evenly spaced. After a couple rows Belle was so smart she knew exactly what to do. I rode for hours and sometimes my legs and siplus would go to sleep.

Dad and Me. Dad taught me farming while riding Belle's back——1940

Dad would have to lift me off the mule when we stopped for a break, 'cuz I could barely walk until my legs woke up. I learned "Gee" for left and "Haw" for right and I learned just how fast the mule would react from verbal commands.

Mr. Moomaw drove a car each day to deliver the kids from off the mountain to the Millstone, where we boarded a school bus for the nine-mile trip to Oldtown. I was a little shy because the kids there seemed to have better clothes than the kids back in West Virginia; seldom did anyone wear clothing with holes in them or shoes that had holes in the soles.

My buddies and me at Oldtown School. My knickers were a catalogue
bargain.——1940
L to r: Tom Santmyire, me, Bill Reckley, Allen Myers and Ray Swick

Mom ordered me some corduroy knickers from Sears, Roebuck. I didn't have problems with wearing clothes with holes, but I didn't much like being the only kid wearing knickers. They made a lot of noise when I walked. And they caused me trouble because I loved to play marbles for keeps. When I kneeled down on my left knee in the wet dirt a big, mud cake would form on the knee of my knickers. The mud cake was formed because I shot from my right knee. I also loved to play mumblety-peg. I was good at making my penknife stick into the ground from my forehead, my nose, my chin, my ear, my shoulder and my elbow. For a while I was the only kid in my group of classmates who could go through all the mumblety-peg positions without a miss—sitting, kneeling and standing. All the boys had penknives either in a case on their hightop shoes or in our pockets and we always played during recess.

My main problem was not the schoolwork, it was getting used to the indoor toilet. The boys would pound on the metal stall partitions and I couldn't go with all that noise going on, and when I would flush the toilet it made a terrific noise as the water rushed through the pot. I personally preferred the outhouses like the one we had at home or like the big outdoor ones we had at school in Springfield, West Virginia.

We received the worst news we had ever received: Tuck came to the house and told us that Dorothy had died. He said that she just suddenly became very weak. Her doctor ordered her to bed and for her to remain flat in bed. The doctor said it was her heart. Dorothy's sisters were taking care of Herbie. Tuck told us that Dorothy died in his arms when she asked him to adjust her pillow a little. Dorothy was the closest person to me that had died, and I had a very difficult time trying to reason why this could happen because she was in her twenties and had a little baby boy. I suppose someday I will get the answer.

6

Sharecropping in Maryland

Five of us—Mom, Jesse, Georgia, Dad and I—were sitting in a circle around a bushel basket. We used it to throw the seed potatoes in after we had split them. Dad was giving instructions on how to cut a whole potato into many small chunks so that each chunk had a robust-looking eye and enough potato body to feed the young potato sprout. We had interesting conversations about the number of potato plants we could get from splitting one potato into many parts. We were all happy that we had accomplished a lot at the new farm place; we were ready to plant field corn, sweet corn, potatoes, bush beans, pole beans, squash, and other truck farm items as well as grain for the animals. Dad said the trick in deciding when to plant is to figure out or guess the proper time, because the soil has to remain warm in order for the seeds to sprout.

"How do you know that the cold weather is over?" I asked.

Dad said, "Generally, when the hickory tree leaves are as large as squirrels' ears it is safe to plant." He added, "The Hagerstown Almanac predicts that it would be safe to plant after May 10 this year, at this latitude and altitude."

Jesse commented, "Those astronomy signs and predictions of when to do things in the soil, as written in the Almanac, are a bunch of bunk according to Mr. House, the FFA and 4-H teacher at school."

Dad had a frown on his face when he said, "Well it was good enough for my father and my father's father, and since Ben Franklin wrote the Almanac, we will use it, and we will plant corn no earlier than May 10." Dad looked at Jesse and said, "You will have to miss about a week of school to help me."

"Isn't there someone else you could ask or hire to help?" Mom asked.

Dad said, "I don't know anyone in these parts well enough to ask and we don't have the money to pay anyone right now. And I need help."

Mom had most of her garden planted. She always set aside the first row next to the lane for her flowers. She used manure from the pile at the barn and was very particular about the manure quality; she didn't want it to be too fresh or hot and she didn't want it to be too old or dried out. She gave instructions just where to get the manure from the pile and how to mix it with the soil. Mom varied the amount of manure for each thing in her garden. She was excited about the annuals coming up around the house—peonies, lily-of-the-valley and roses. She told us, "The lady who lived here before me also loved flowers, so I will do my best to keep them nice."

We had two orchards, about 100 apple trees and 75 peach trees. Right now the fruit on the trees was marble size, bigger than a peewee marble and not as big as a plunk marble. Examining the fruit closely, Dad noticed that small mites, which he called aphids, were starting to eat the new leaves and the leaves were curling. He got the wagon-mounted, one-cylinder, gasoline-engine-powered sprayer and mixed 50 gallons of chemicals. He used water from the barn reservoir to fill the sprayer.

Me, a want-to-be hay rake operator—1941

We had to use a screen to filter out the tadpoles and other water critters that came out of the pipe. Jesse harnessed the mules to pull the sprayer and Dad told me to lead Beck while he led Jack. But when Jack heard the noisy engine on the sprayer he began to pull back and wanted to head for the barn. Dad tried to hook him to the sprayer but he was scared to death from the noise so Dad said, "Harness up Belle. This contrary bastard won't settle down." Jesse harnessed Belle and hitched her to the sprayer. When we got to the orchard and started spraying, both the mules were frightened from the racket made by the high-pressure spray nozzle. Dad had me stand in front and hold the mules. I pulled some fresh grass and started feeding them, but Dad yelled, "Don't feed them grass! This spray is poison and it will make them sick or kill them."

Later on, Dad mowed a large field and after the grass had dried for about two days it became hay. He used the mules to pull a hay rake that shaped the hay into windrows and after that, Jesse and I used pitchforks to pile the hay into stacks. Dad showed me how to use the pitchfork to shape the hay in such a way that when it was thrown onto the stack it formed a watershed that could turn the rain off the stack rather than letting the rain soak into it. We used Belle to pull the stacks into the haymow by wrapping a log chain around the bottom of each stack and dragging the stack to the barn. Throwing the hay up into the haymow was a tough job for me; this was the hardest I had ever worked.

Everything that Dad had planted soon needed cultivating and he and Jesse were working from before sunup to dark every day. The insects were eating the vegetables. We sprayed and dusted, but some of the chemicals were not doing the job. Using a coffee can with about two inches of kerosene in it, Mom and I crawled along the rows of potato plants and knocked potato bugs into the can. Large green worms with horns were also eating up our tomato plants. These worms could destroy a plant in a single day. We had to look carefully to see the worms for they were the same color as the plants; we used pliers to pull the worms from the plants, and smashed them.

After a while our green beans, squash, cucumbers, radishes and eggplant were ready for market. Mom and I picked the vegetables and once a week Dad made a trip to Cumberland to sell them. Mr. Millholland suggested that if Dad would drive the truck slowly in the Green Street section of Cumberland and yell, "farm-fresh vegetables," people would buy directly from the back of the truck and we could sell at a higher price than the larger markets would pay. We did this and sold out within a couple of hours each time we took a load in to town. Jesse and I would run from the truck to the houses and deliver the vegetables. Sometimes we received tips and it sure beat working in the fields. Sweet corn, cantaloupes, watermelons and tomatoes were big sellers. People began watching for us and they would come out of their homes to buy from the truck. We tried to set the same hours each week and Dad said we were really doing well with the truck garden and getting good money hustling the vegetables.

After the truck gardening was over the hardest part was yet to come: cutting field corn and putting it in shocks. Digging the potatoes was hard, too. We used a single-blade plow pulled by a mule to cut a deep furrow in the potato rows to turn the potatoes out of the ground. We crawled along the rows, pulling a basket that we loaded with potatoes until it was full. Dad allowed Jesse to drive the truck in the field and he loaded the baskets into the truck.

Local folks were beginning to come to our place to buy field corn and potatoes. Dad was working into the night by lantern, shucking corn. Jesse was able to help but I wasn't very useful at shucking corn. My hands became so sore that they bled; Dad and Jesse's hands had deep calluses. We hauled the cornstalks to the barn and chopped them into short pieces for the cows to eat as fodder in winter.

When fall came it was time to start school. I had grown taller and stronger from working during the summer, and I was glad to start third grade. I liked Miss Carter, my third grade teacher, a lot because she allowed anyone who finished the classroom assignments early to work on projects. While we were studying about Eskimos I made igloos out of a salt and flour mixture. I loved school again and everything was going great. Some of my new friends, Bill Reckley and his older brother Hartley, and Gladstone Beeler, lived three or four miles from me. We had a great time at school and were able to get together after Sunday school and every now and then on Saturdays.

Dad——John Russell Shipe, heir to the soil——1941

Dad took the wheat and buckwheat down to Mr. Taschenberger's mill and had it ground. Mom made buckwheat pancakes, which we all loved. When I prepared the food for the hogs we mixed the ground wheat in water. I liked to dip my fingers into the middling and eat the raw, dry meal, the part of the wheat grain that we made into hog feed. Mr. Taschenberger said that middling was the best part of the wheat grain; the white part that people used for bread had much less nourishment. Another of my favorite snacks was raw rolled oats.

I was being given more chores to do, because Jesse was expected to do the work of a man and Dad had plenty for him to do. My sister, Georgia, did house chores like cleaning the kerosene lamp and lantern globes and helping Mom with washing, ironing and housecleaning. She was not happy at school and neither was Jesse.

One day Mom noticed that my skin color was not right and asked me how I felt. I told her I was tired and not feeling very strong. She put her hand on my forehead and said I had a fever. When I got to school a teacher took my temperature and told me I should see a doctor. Mom and Dad took me to Memorial Hospital in Cumberland. The doctor couldn't find anything wrong with me by looking in my eyes and throat and tapping on me so he said he wanted to place me under observation and I was admitted to the hospital.

The nurses took my clothes and shoes, gave me a gown that was sort of like a girl's outfit, and put me in a bed. They said that I could not get out of bed even to go to the bathroom and I was not to leave the room. A nurse brought a porcelain jug with a handle on it, slipped it under the sheet and put my dinkus in it and said, "Pee for me."

I said, "I can't go with you looking at me." She left and I went a little bit in the jug, for I wasn't sure whether I could shut it off without overflowing the jug.

I was scared because this was the first time I would be sleeping away from home and alone in a strange place. I was in a room that had four beds and three were empty. Mom came to visit me. She said that the doctor asked a lot of questions and he thought maybe I had Rabbit Fever or Bang's Disease or even some other kind of fever since we lived in the country and drank raw cow's milk and maybe I had been playing with rabbits and other animals and caught something from them. I told Mom that this place was spooky enough and I didn't want to worry about all those weird diseases. Anyhow, there wasn't anything wrong with Grannie's milk. As Mom was leaving she said she would only be able to come to town and see me every third day. I told her not to worry, for I was feeling better already.

The only way I could let the nurses know I wanted them was to ring a bell that was like the round bell Miss Carter, my teacher, had on her desk. When they turned out the lights I rang the bell and the nurse came. I was too embarrassed to tell her I was afraid to be in the room alone so I told her I had to poop and she gave me a bedpan and I didn't do anything in the pan. When the nurse came for the bedpan she said, "Don't fake that you need something again, for I won't come." She turned out the lights and left the room.

The next day I was so bored I could barely stand it. Late in the afternoon the nurses wheeled a little boy into the room and put him kitty-cornered from me. They pulled my curtain but there was an open space big enough that I could watch what was going on. You could tell they had a lot to do for the boy because they were coming and going every couple minutes. The nurses told me that I was on a liquid diet and the only food I could have was broth and all the water I could drink. That didn't bother me because I wasn't hungry.

About dark more and more things were happening around the boy's bed. The nurses wheeled in a large green cylinder and put hoses to his nose. Soon the boy's parents came and the doctors and nurses became even busier. They used a wrench to pound on the green tank, and they began calling out to the boy in loud voices. Soon a preacher came and prayed with the parents right outside my curtain, and I could tell that the preacher believed God was going to take care of everything. Two doctors were talking to the parents; they told them that their son was more seriously ill than they thought and he was not responding to medicine. The mother began to scream and holler and her husband and the preacher had their hands full trying to settle her down. A couple hours later, the doctor told the parents that their son was dead, and the mother was screaming for her baby to come back and the preacher was praying a very long prayer and asking God to send the Holy Spirit for into His hands we give his soul.

Soon they disconnected the hoses and placed a sheet over the boy's head and wheeled him out of the room. Someone dimmed the lights and I was scared. During this whole time none of the nurses checked on me. I began to pray my prayer, "Now I lay me down to sleep, I pray the Lord my soul to keep, and if I should die before I wake, I pray the Lord my soul to take." And I asked God about the Holy Spirit that the preacher was asking to come to get the soul of the little boy, and I let God know that the little boy wasn't in this room any longer and please don't make a mistake.

This was the first time in all my born days that I stayed awake all night, and in the morning I was exhausted. Sometime around eight a nurse came in and asked me if I had eliminated since I arrived in the hospital. I asked what she meant about elimination and she told me what she meant and I said, "No." She came back with a little white bucket that she hung on the wall and said she was going to give me an enema by putting a tube in my butt and allowing some soapy liquid to drain into me to clean me out for an X-ray. She started working on my rear end and I clinched tight and she yelled at me to relax, but I couldn't. Then she asked, "When was the last time that you pooped?" I said, "I can't remember." She took off out of my room and soon she had two other nurses helping her and they were picking at my bottom and I heard something that sounded like rocks hitting the bottom of the bedpan. I yelled and told them how much it hurt but they just kept on picking. The older nurse said, "You have compacted bowels and this is the worst case I've ever seen. You will just have to hold on and bear it, for we have to dig the stuff out of you."

The nurses left me alone for a short time but came back and continued the probing and picking. They tried to use the enema thing but it didn't do the job. They would work on me and then let me rest for a while. They began to give me some type of medicine that I had a terrible time getting down. The doctor came into my room and the first thing he did was push real hard on my lower stomach. I screamed like I was being killed. He said, "You have compacted bowels. What have you been eating?" I told him about eating middlings and rolled oats and he said, "This is a very serious problem and you will have to bear with the nurses while they clean you out."

I was putting two and two together and decided that if they rolled the green cylinder into my room, I was going to run out of the hospital and thumb a ride to Spring Gap and walk up the mountain. I tried to stay awake to guard against them doing anything more, but I fell asleep. The next day the nurses began working on me again, following the same procedure they had used the day before.

Mom came to see me and said, "Plumb my soul to goodness, why didn't you tell me that you weren't going?"

I said, "Well I didn't like to go at school and I suppose that one thing led to another and here I am, bound up tighter than a fat wood tick. Will the doctor let me go home?"

Mom replied, "No, the doctor doesn't know when you can go home. This is a very serious illness. They will have to continue cleaning you out and then your intestines will have to heal. You still have a fever and that means you have infection in your intestines and all that has to heal."

I told mom about the little boy dying in this very room and from my experience I had figured out that this room was only for those that were going to die. She assured me by saying, "They put you in this room to isolate you from the others because of the unknown cause of your fever and as soon as they are sure the fever is from the infection of your intestines they will put you in a room with others."

A week later, I was wheeled into a room with other kids. I was allowed to use a wheel chair to get around. I drove the nurses nuts riding the chair up and down the hall. On my nineteenth day in the hospital I was served my first solid food, a single graham cracker, and when I practically begged for another the nurses wouldn't give it to me. Over the next day or two the food supply increased. The food tasted different. I loved the fresh vegetables, green beans, and carrots that came on my tray, even though I had never been fond of vegetables. I asked for more food, but the nurses said that I was on portion control, whatever that meant.

On the twenty-first day after my admittance to the hospital, Mom and Dad came to get me and I was so glad to be going home. I was very weak and it seemed that all the strength I had gained during the summer was gone.

It was my first day back at school. I entered Miss Carter's room and couldn't believe my eyes—there was a new boy at my desk. He had his knees on the seat and was leaning over and talking to my girl, Ruth Snider. I went right up and asked him who he thought he was using my desk and sharing my comic books with my girl. He said, "It is none of your business. I was assigned to sit here." We began to tussle and Miss Carter grabbed us both and that saved him. She introduced me to Kenneth Cage and said that he had been sitting in my desk while I was away. She later assigned him to another desk. We had gotten off to a bad start, but since his name was Kenneth I figured that we had one thing in common. We talked together at lunch. He had a store-bought bread sandwich with bologna, my favorite. I traded him my homemade bread and sugar-cured ham sandwich and we shared a slice of Mom's homemade apple pie.

Since it was winter, Dad had more time to spend around the house. He wanted all of us to have a good Christmas and a nice tree so he got the ax and he asked me to go with him to the woods to find a tree. It had snowed a little the evening before and Dad delighted in teaching me how to track rabbits or other animal tracks in the snow. He was able to predict which side of a tree or brush pile or other covering where the critters or the rabbit would hide. He told me that the rabbit would be sitting out of the wind, you could always count on that, and that the rabbit would detect the scent and sound before we came too close. If you make too much noise or if he could smell you he would scoot out of harm's way and be gone.

We found a beautiful cedar tree and Dad cut it. He said that removing the cedar tree served two purposes: one was to be a Christmas tree and the other was to get rid of a problem because cedar trees carried a rust that was infecting apple trees and caused a brown scale on the fruit.

On Christmas Eve the bare tree was in the living room and after we had eaten supper Dad said he would go to the Millstone and get a newspaper and some snuff. Mom asked him to get a few things, one of which was molasses. Dad was late getting back from the store and I could hear Mom and him arguing about the molasses. He had bought a gallon of sorghum molasses and we all hated the strong taste of the stuff, but he loved it. What the fuss really was about was that Dad had imbibed three or four beers and Mom was on to him about it. When Dad climbed into bed he immediately fell asleep and snored so loud I couldn't tell if Mom was trimming the tree or not.

Christmas morning was beautiful; the tree was trimmed and gifts were under it. One gift that the whole family appreciated was a Philco battery-powered radio. When we got it on the table and connected the A and B batteries, Dad turned it on and found the strongest station, WTBO in Cumberland. We had Christmas music as we opened our gifts. I got the dual-wheeled American Flyer wagon with wooden racks that I had asked for and another gift that I didn't expect, my very own Bible. It had a genuine leather cover. Mom said I should start Sunday school at Mount Tabor Church and all I had to do was be out at the road on Sunday morning and Mr. Columbus Delauder would pick any of us up and bring us home after church.

I remember that Christmas well.

7

Good times on Martins Mountain

The New Year of 1941 began with a fluffy three-inch snowfall. After the weather cleared and the sun was out bright it became one of those days that stick in your mind, when the snow that covered everything muffled sounds of early morning. I stood on the back porch and looked into the valley below and took in the beauty and was glad that we lived in such a beautiful place. Inside, Mom was preparing a breakfast of ham and eggs with fresh-baked biscuits.

Around the table we were making comments about the good year that we just had and how all the hard work had paid off. We wanted to boast about how wonderful things were compared to just eight months earlier; you could sense that each of us wanted to rejoice, but as I looked into my family's eyes I saw fear. It was fear that it wouldn't last; so we didn't talk about it in boastful terms.

Jesse milked the cows, Grannie and Nellie, inside the barn during the winter. I scooped grain from the feed barrels and placed it in the trough and threw down hay for the cows and mules. The animals went for the grain first thing, and then they would munch on the hay. Jesse was singing as he milked; the cows really liked that. Mom told us that singing helped the cows give their milk. Some people even played the radio in their barns and their milk production increased. Jesse also had a habit of squirting milk to the barn cats. There were three cats lined up along the wall and he would squirt warm milk at their heads, and they licked their whiskers and their fur and then each other to get the milk.

This one particular morning when Jesse and I returned from the barn, we noticed that Mom had her nice dress on with a full apron and she had finished most of her morning chores early and she seemed happy as a lark. Jesse said, "It's not Sunday and you have a nice dress on, what's up?"

Mom waiting in the snow for her ride to Spring Gap Ladies Homemakers
Club meeting—1941

She replied, "Mrs. Miller and Mrs. Twigg are going to pick me up and we're going to the Spring Gap Ladies Homemakers Club meeting."

"What's that all about?" Jesse inquired.

Mom answered, "It's where ladies in the area get together and work on projects that will make homemaking easier for all of us. It will be my first meeting."

This was the first year that I had made a New Year's resolution. I resolved that I would be out by the road each Sunday morning to wait for a ride and go to Sunday school and church at Mt. Tabor Methodist with the neighbors that lived above us. When I mentioned this to Mom, she was delighted and indicated that she wanted to go. Each Sunday we were both up and out by the road; generally, Columbus Delauder would pick us up, but if he weren't going he would make sure the Twiggs or the Parks would stop for us.

I had looked through my new Bible and couldn't find a chapter on prayer. Being able to pray is what I wanted to know more about. My nighttime prayer was simple and I believed God heard it and answered it, but I knew there had to be more to praying than my bedtime prayer and the Lord's Prayer we said at Oldtown School. I figured that Sunday school would have a class on prayer, but after a month I saw that all of the lessons were from Bible stories. Mr. Delauder was my Sunday school teacher; he taught the boys. My good friends, Bill and Hartley

Reckley, were in my class and I learned that their father, Merle, was the preacher when the regular preacher wasn't there. The regular preacher had other churches to attend to and he was only at our church one week a month.

Reverend Reckley had a good prayer at the end of his sermons, but that prayer was for everyone and I wanted a special one for me. I liked Reverend Reckley's sermons, for he would pick a word like grace and talk about grace, how God was full of it and He wanted everyone to receive His Grace, which He freely gave if you asked for it. Grace was something that could not be worked for and God had total control of who received it and whomever He favored received it freely from Him. These messages persuaded me to listen to sermons.

I liked the preaching because I could ponder what was said for a whole week. I seldom talked to anyone about liking sermons, because adults always would tell me to be good and everything would be all right. But by listening to sermons I came to the conclusion that it was most important to recognize who God was and if anything good was going to come into my life it came from Him and the bad stuff was when I chose my own way.

I had never had a birthday party, but this year, I received something on my birthday that I had been wanting ever since I had seen it advertised in a Captain Marvel comic book: a Red Ryder beebee gun and a giant box of beebees. The rifle had a ring on the side with a genuine leather thong tied to it and *"Red Ryder"* etched into the metal. Mom said that it was a gift from her and dad as well as Lena and Betty. I headed to the barn and waited for mice to come out near the grain barrel where grain had been spilled. I remained absolutely still and it wasn't long before the mice appeared. At the supper table I was able to report on my good hunting and that I had killed almost a dozen mice. Everyone was proud of me for killing the rodents for it was a good deed to get rid of the mice.

My sister Betty announced that she and Buss Seville, who lived in Romney, West Virginia, were getting married and that after their honeymoon they would be coming to the mountain to visit. Betty had been staying at Lena and Robert Lee's apartment in Romney while she finished high school. Mom thought that Buss was a good catch for Betty because his family was well known and his father was the Buick dealer and he also owned a beverage distributorship.

When Betty and Buss arrived on the mountain after their honeymoon the first thing that Buss did was open the trunk of his 1941 Buick convertible and presented me with his 40-pound pull archery set, complete with a quiver full of practice arrows, six hunting arrows, forearm protector, a finger glove, a nice round straw-filled target and extra target covers. I couldn't string the bow so Buss showed me how to hold the bow against my foot for stringing. He also taught me a lot about shooting the bow and arrow; he had been taught to shoot when he attended Virginia Military Institute. Jesse also liked the bow and arrow. He could really pull the arrows back and when the arrows hit the target the arrow would go through the straw. I practiced shooting every chance I got and between the bee-bee gun, the archery set, a .22 rifle, a .410 and 12-gauge shotgun, I had a great deal of fun.

We had a May Day program at school and I had a part in wrapping the May-pole. Miss Carter explained what we were to do but we never practiced. I had my piece of yellow crepe paper and when the music began people started to circle the pole, soon everyone was confused and we ended up with a big mess. I was embarrassed and some of the girls were so embarrassed that they went off and cried. I felt almost bad enough to cry.

Miss Carter told me before she gave out report cards that I would pass to the fourth grade and that she was proud of the way that I had been able to miss over three weeks of school when I was in the hospital and catch up with the class.

I loved school more than any other thing. I especially loved the bus ride from Spring Gap to Oldtown School. I sat with various friends, and liked sitting with the girls the most. I had one big problem: I was not good at getting a conversation going and when I talked about my beebee gun or archery set or how good I was at shooting things—the girls didn't care. I had already learned not to talk about butchering hogs, killing mice, shooting and skinning rabbits, eating squirrels and the like. The girls would start to squirm and turn their noses up like they didn't want any part of what I was doing.

Aunt Beulah, Mom's sister who everyone called "Boots," wrote to Mom that she and her daughter, Dottie Ann, who was one year younger than me, were coming from Akron, Ohio, to spend a couple weeks with us and attend the Shipe reunion at Uncle Ed's up in Frostburg, Maryland. Mom was excited about this; she began planning for their arrival and how she and her other sisters, Nellie and Ella, could get together down in Springfield. Boots also wrote that she'd like me to visit in Akron.

Mr. Millholland came out from Cumberland in his big Caddy, dressed in a suit, vest, tie and hat, as usual. I tagged along with him and Dad as they walked to see the fields and the peach and apple orchards. The fruit had set real well, about one-half to three-quarters of an inch in diameter, and there wasn't any evidence of severe insect damage or blight like last year. Dad showed him how he thinned the fruit to allow three to four inches between each piece. Mr. Millholland looked astonished at the amount of fruit that had to be removed. The trees in some places had fruit packed together along the limbs looking more like grapes than apples and peaches. Mr. Millholland asked, "How are you sure that the fruit that remains will mature?" Dad answered, "You simply try to judge the best of the best and hope that you made the right choice."

Dad pointed to some black clouds that were gathering and said, "On top of this mountain in June you had better keep an eye on the sky, for the storms could roll in and the lightning is very dangerous. And from the looks of the sky we had better head for shelter." As soon as we reached the porch of the old middle house, we heard a loud "Whack!" on the tin roof of the back porch and a large hailstone rolled off onto the grass. It was followed by more and more and the noise was so loud that Mr. Millholland removed his hearing aids and held his ears.

The hailstorm went on for a while and the lightning was striking all around and the thunder was echoing through the valley below. Lightning hit one of the sweet cherry trees near the porch. The tree split wide open and pieces of bark landed near Mr. Millholland.

When the storm moved away, we found the ground covered with hailstones. One look at the grape arbor showed the magnitude of the damage: leaves were stripped from the grape vines and the peach and cherry trees. The fruit was either knocked off or had severe damage. Mr. Millholland put his hearing aids back into his ears and spoke softly as he questioned Dad about the condition of his orchards, and they both concluded that it wouldn't pay to walk to the orchard, for it was certain that the fruit crop for this year would not be marketable. The hail had stripped clean the trees around the house where we were standing.

Mr. Millholland walked slowly to his car and as he stood there I noted his eyes were watery and he looked at Dad and began telling him about his son, Captain Randolph Millholland Jr., who was on a special assignment in France. He said that he had received a telegram that his son had been wounded. He was carried from the beach at Dunkirk, France, and transported to England in a small boat by English civilians. He was alive but in critical condition in a hospital. Mr. Millholland said he was never happy that his son was a member of the U.S. Army Rangers.

After Mr. Millholland left Dad told Mom that he felt that Mr. Millholland seemed to have lost his love for farming and owning an orchard. She said, "He had too much of a burden to carry, with the condition of his son and dealing with the risks of losing money in farming and owning an orchard." And she asked, "We aren't at war, why was Randy wounded on that beach in France?"

Dad couldn't answer except to say that he heard on the radio that the Germans pushed allied forces out of France and many were killed.

We all went in different directions to check on the animals and determine any other damage from the storm. I went to the hog pen and found the hogs glad to see me. They had huddled into a corner of their pen with their butts against the fence and when they saw me they started to move toward the trough. The final report was that the animals were okay, but the buildings that didn't have metal roofs had a lot of damage and would leak until repaired. Dad believed that some of the crops had a chance of making it since they were just breaking through the ground.

Doc Tashenberger told Dad that his father was closing down his mill in Spring Gap and the best place to get feed supplies would be at the Southern States Cooperative Feed Store in Cumberland, directly across the railroad tracks from the Queen City train station. So Dad joined the Co-Op, which meant that he would receive a discount on his purchases. Dad liked the location of the Southern States store because he was able to park his pickup there and he and Mom could walk to Baltimore Street to shop; he hated the traffic downtown.

Mom, Jesse, Georgia and I had a difficult time convincing Dad that we should go to town on a particular Saturday evening and see *Gone with the Wind* at the Strand Theater. When we got out of the four-hour movie show it was dark and Dad was fit to be tied, for he had sat in the truck and waited for us. He hated driving in the dark. I noted that he had had a couple of beers. We got in the truck and headed for Spring Gap. As we moved along Route 51 out of Cumberland the six-volt headlights on the truck were so dim that a flashlight would have given more light. Dad drove very slowly. At Mexico Farms, a fog bank began to form and as we got nearer the river it was really bad. Jesse and I stood up in the back of the truck and watched for anything in the highway. We entered the Western Maryland Railroad underpass and as the pickup was coming out of the tunnel—"WHAM!" Our truck hit something, skidded sideways and came to a stop against the guardrails. Jesse and I were almost thrown from the back of the truck. Dad had hit a stake-body truck that had stopped with its lights off on the highway. Dad ran up to the truck and yelled at the driver, but he wasn't in the truck or anywhere to be found. The only damage to our truck was the driver's-side door hinge. The door hinge was bent so that we couldn't open the door. There wasn't any damage to the big truck. Dad had to scoot across the passenger side to get to the driver's seat. We continued to creep home in the fog. We all knew that it would be a long time before Dad would take us to town for an evening show.

The Consolidated Orchard Company had a bunkhouse for men about two miles beyond our house and often men looking for work would walk the road to the foreman's house and if they weren't hired they would stop by our place on their way off the mountain and ask about work. Sometimes Dad would hire a man for a short time. Generally, these men only needed a little money to get them to another place to look for a job. The men helped a lot to relieve my dad's burden.

One day an elderly gentleman stopped and introduced himself as Mr. Dunham and said he needed a place to stay and a job. Dad hired him even though he was pretty feeble and wasn't able to work a team in the fields. Dad gave him the job of pulling weeds in Mom's garden. Usually, hired hands never ate at our house, but Mr. Dunham was different; he took his meals with us. He was a frail person and Mom fed him plenty and he was very grateful. He never talked about his family. He fixed a pad for sleeping in a dry place he found in the old, middle house.

One day I saw Jesse and Dad running through the cantaloupe patch and then I saw that Mr. Dunham was lying on the ground. Jesse picked him up and he and Dad put him in the pickup and headed for the hospital. In about four hours Jesse and Dad returned and said that Mr. Dunham had died. The doctors couldn't do anything for him because a blood artery in his stomach had burst and he bled to death. The next day Mom and Dad gathered up his things, put them in a paper sack and took them to Cumberland where Mr. Dunham was buried. Mom and Dad and some graveyard workers were the only people at the burial.

The summer was passing too fast for me, and the time was close for my trip to Akron. August arrived and there I was with Mom at the Queen City train station in Cumberland, with the big passenger train coming into Track 1 with its bell ringing and the steam hissing out near the engine's front wheels. The Pullman cars were near the front of the train. A porter asked Mom where we were going and she told him I was going to Akron, by myself, and he said, "This is the car, and I will take good care of the boy."

He said to me, "My name is Andy."

I said, "Hi, my name is Kenneth."

From inside the railcar, I looked out the window and saw Mom on the platform waving. The thought hit me: Oh, my Lord. I'm alone and going hundreds of miles away and I didn't know how to tell when to get off the train. I asked Andy about that and he said he would awake me in plenty of time to eat breakfast and get off the train in Akron. I had never trusted a stranger before and I was plenty worried about whether Andy could be trusted for he was black and I had never personally had any direct dealings with a black man before.

When the train began to move, fear came over me and I knew that only God could settle my nerves. Soon we were heading out of the station and into the Narrows Gap. The B & O tracks went along Wills Creek where Lover's Leap was and Uncle Mac and Aunt Nellie lived nearby in Locust Grove. The train began to pick up speed and the telephone poles became a blur and the clicking sounds of the wheels hitting the cracks in the steel rails grew closer and closer together. As it became dark outside I saw my reflection in the window and I talked to myself a little. My stomach was still in knots. Andy and another man in uniform came by, punching tickets, and Andy asked, "Do you want to go to the dining car and have dinner?"

I said, "I'm not hungry."

He said, "You could have dinner for about $2.50."

I said, "I have a five spot, but I don't want to spend it on supper."

Andy pulled down my bed from overhead, closed a curtain, told me where the toilet was, and said that when I was ready I could go to bed. He suggested that that would be a good thing for me to do because he didn't want to catch me wandering in the aisle. He said he would put me off the train if I went between cars.

I slipped off my shoes and crawled into bed and this was a whole new experience for me. The train was rocking and even though the bed had a sideboard I still felt like I would roll out. I said my nighttime prayer and began thinking about home, the mules, the cows and Queenie our dog, her pups, and everyone at home. I was also concerned about oversleeping and having to continue on to wherever the train went. When I saw Andy through the crack in the curtain I asked, "What would happen if I missed getting off in Akron?"

He said, "Cleveland was the next large city after Akron and not to worry, he would get me up and off the train." Andy also said, "Now if you don't quit worrying me about getting off the train I will put you off in Pittsburgh and send you back to Cumberland."

The next morning, Andy gave me a shake and told me I should get up and eat breakfast. He suggested a glass of orange juice and some dry cereal with cream. I spent $1 for breakfast and vowed to myself that that would be the last time I would spend so much on so little food.

When the train stopped Andy helped me off with my bag and as soon as I hit the platform, Aunt Boots yelled, "Over here, Buddy!" She grabbed me and gave me a big hug and Dottie Ann did the same. I loaded my bag in the trunk of their maroon 1940 Ford sedan and we started toward their house. I felt sick and I asked aunt Boots, "Please stop, I have to throw up." When I got back into the car Aunt Boots said, "Do you continue to have problems like when you were in the hospital?"

I answered, "No, my problem is that I try to keep all my exciting experiences inside and when I get real full it just runs out. I'll be okay now."

Aunt Boots had a full week planned for me: a trip to Cuyahoga Falls amusement park where there was a giant roller coaster, a trip to a farm that Dottie Ann's uncle owned in Wooster, Ohio, and a trip to Cleveland and Lake Erie. Also, we would go to the Soapbox Derby. Dottie Ann let me know that they planned a party at their house and many of her friends from school would be there and we would be attending Mass. I asked her what Mass was and she said a service at her church.

The roller coaster ride at the amusement park was the biggest thrill I had ever had. We rode on Lake Erie in a speedboat and that was super; the lake was so wide I couldn't see across it. The farm in Wooster was huge; it had at least two tractors and a lot of farm machines. Our fields at home were very small compared to the Ohio fields. The kids who raced their soapbox cars sure were anxious. Uncle Frank was able to get us close to where the kids were wiping their cars and getting them weighed and inspected. Three cars at a time were released at the top of the hill and each winner was returned to the top for another heat until they determined the national champion of the 48 states.

Aunt Boots checked me over good before we got in the car to go to Sunday Mass. She said the Catholic Church was different from the Methodist Church; they kneeled a lot and if I watched Dottie Ann, I would get along fine. Hundreds of people filled the huge church. Everyone stood when the service began and the organ began to play. I had never heard such a robust sound. Some boys dressed in robes came down the aisle and many robed men followed. One had a little bucket that smoked. The preacher, who I learned was a priest, was so far away that I could barely see him over the adults' heads. I noticed that everyone had a little book and followed the priest as he spoke in Latin. I felt embarrassed about not knowing when to stand and when to sit or kneel so I kept my head down most of the time. I didn't understand anything that was happening and I was relieved when it was over.

At Dottie Ann's party there must have been about 20 kids, mostly girls. The priest who did the Mass and another priest come by and Aunt Boots introduced me to them. They were nice men. Shortly after we had eaten the food that Aunt Boots had fixed, Dottie Ann got her friends into a circle with a Coca-Cola bottle in the middle. She gave the bottle a spin and it stopped at the boy next to me and she gave him a big kiss. I couldn't believe my eyes—kissing with someone watching! The boy spun the bottle and it stopped at a girl and he kissed her. I was getting very uncomfortable and planning what I was going to do so I wouldn't get kissed. Then the bottle stopped, and it pointed at me—and it took my breath away. The girl who had spun it came running toward me and everyone was screaming and I took off up the basement steps and through the house, and I scooted under the glider on the front porch. All the girls were chasing me now and they pushed the glider back and began to kiss me and I was so embarrassed. The more I resisted, the more they kissed me, so I quit resisting and then they quit kissing me. I wouldn't go back to the party until many of the kids came up and explained that the game was all in fun and they played it at every party. They asked me to rejoin them and said "spin-the-bottle" was over. I finally did go back downstairs to the party.

Aunt Boots and Dottie Ann got me to the train station in Akron early in the morning and saw me off. I felt very confident about riding the train to Cumberland for it would be mostly a daylight trip. I had plenty of time to ponder all that I had seen and done on my trip; I felt like I was more experienced. Mom and Jesse met me and they wanted to hear about what I had done.

Miss Beck, my fourth-grade teacher, had black hair and kept her fingernails polished. She seemed to glide around the classroom and was very helpful when kids raised their hands. Kenneth Cage wore suspenders and I thought that to be a little unusual—until a spitball hit me up beside the head. I looked over and he was having a lot of fun shooting spitballs using his elastic suspenders. When I got home I put in for a pair of suspenders, making a solid case for needing them to keep my pants up. Mom got me a pair and then Kenneth and I both began having fun shooting spitballs. It wasn't long until many of the boys recognized the benefits of being fashionable and wore suspenders. Miss Beck caught Kenneth shooting the spitballs. I was hoping she would make him take them off and he would have to hold his pants up all day, but she didn't.

On December 7 we heard on the radio about airplanes bombing Pearl Harbor. We didn't know how far away Pearl Harbor was and the whole family was scared about our military men being killed and we listened to so much news on the radio that the batteries went dead. Dad went straight to town on Monday and got new batteries and we had the news on when president Roosevelt declared war on Japan, Germany and Italy, the Axis enemy.

8

Fire on the mountain

Mom was worrying more and more each day about the war and such. She was convinced that what was predicted in the Bible about the end of the world was going to happen soon and that the world would likely be consumed by fire. She was afraid that the enemy bombers that were bombing our Allied Forces would soon begin dropping bombs on Cumberland and eventually our place on the mountain. She was not sleeping well and none of the family knew enough about what was happening in the world to give her any peace.

The preacher at church was also preaching on "The End Times," "Repentance from Sins" and the need for "Salvation." I could tell that church attendance was improving and many talked about a period of Hell on earth. All of the messages that we were hearing were warning people that the world's problems were due to the sins of the people.

We were having more revival services in the churches from Oldtown to Cumberland. One evening Columbus Delauder invited me to a revival service at Davis Memorial Methodist Church. He said that he would take any of the guys in his Sunday school class who wanted to go. This church was located about half way between Spring Gap and Cumberland on Route 51, an area called Mexico Farms. Anytime someone offered a ride off the mountain, I was ready to go, especially if other kids were involved. Church was one place I was sure that Mom and Dad would give me permission to go. I had been to several revival services, and I didn't expect the one at Davis Memorial Church would be any different than the others, for the church was in the same circuit as our church, Mt. Tabor Methodist at Spring Gap. The church was large and made of brick; it could hold about 80 people without extra chairs. It wasn't long before they gathered the young people in from playing outside and made sure that we had seats near the front. On this particular night the church was packed. The preacher's theme was "All had sinned and fallen short of the Glory of God." He said, "No matter what you did or intended to do, if you died without Jesus Christ living in your heart you were going to spend eternity in hell." At the end of the message the preacher had a prayer that obviously was directed at me. I could tell, even with my eyes closed, that people were going toward the altar and that the prayer wouldn't end as long as people were moving forward.

We were instructed to keep our heads bowed and our eyes closed, but I sneaked a peek every now and then, and people continued going forward. I had the feeling that I was the only young person remaining in the pews. I also felt it was time for me to settle this issue, but just as I was about to make a move, a man put his hand on my shoulder, squeezed pretty hard, and whispered in my ear, "Is there any reason why you shouldn't accept Jesus as your Savior?" I didn't answer him and before I knew it, I was up the aisle and kneeling at the altar. I verbally committed myself to God based upon what His son Jesus had done for me, giving His life and shedding His blood and paying the price for my sin. I felt assured that I was forgiven, God had forgiven me and viewed me as if I had never sinned, placing my sin upon Jesus; and further, according to Scripture he wasn't going to bring the past sins issue up again.

During our ride home nothing was said about the altar call or who went up or who didn't. But I sensed that the relationship between us boys would never be the same. We weren't able to express what or why we did what we did, let alone whether we knew how to act as Christians. One thing for sure, if the bombs fell on our house and killed me I knew where I would spend eternity.

I told Mom what I had done and she was happy for me and she told me that she had been praying for me to make a decision for a long time.

I decided to pay more attention to helping Mom for it was becoming obvious that her work around the home never ended. I asked her what I could do to help and she said that on washdays I could build fires under the two black iron washpots and fill them with water so that she could transfer the hot water to her washing machine in the basement. I wanted to help her right away, so I grabbed a bucket to start filling the pots, but she stopped me and informed me that the water would freeze overnight and the swelling of the ice would crack the cast-iron pots.

I was up earlier than usual to keep my new commitment. The pitcher pump outside over the cistern was frozen, and it required hot water to be poured into the suction part of the pump to melt the ice inside. I got the hot water from the kitchen stove reservoir. I was able to pump enough water to fill the two 10-gallon pots. Building a fire was a snap for I had plenty of rich pine kindling split up behind the kitchen stove.

Even though filling the pots with water was a lot of help to Mom she would have to carry the hot water from the pots to her washing machine in the basement.

A one-cylinder gasoline engine powered the washing machine and wringer, and Mom complained that Satan himself lived in that engine. Many times she would use the kick-starter until she gave out and would then have to do the entire wash on a scrub board. Often she would hang the clothes on the clothesline outside and they would freeze stiffer than a board and the clothes would have to remain there until the weather warmed to melt the ice so that the clothes would dry.

This was my best school year ever. Mrs. Harris was a great fifth-grade teacher and I worked hard to learn as much as possible and do well on her examinations. There was mention by some that I was the teacher's pet, but I didn't care. My grades improved to where I was receiving excellent on all my subjects and I had perfect attendance, but Mrs. Harris marked on my report card that my behavior required improvement and gave me a couple "U" marks. I couldn't understand how having fun was so unsatisfactory.

The State of Maryland required every fifth-grader to take a battery of multiple-choice tests covering all subjects and we spent a full day taking them. Mrs. Harris got the results of the tests back after a couple of weeks and I was one of six people in the class to receive a superior grade. She said that we were ranked high among all of the kids from the whole state and she was very proud of us.

Mrs. Harris was teaching ancient history at school, but due to the war she shortened that study and began teaching world geography. We kids all wanted to know more and more about where Germany, Italy and Japan were on the map. Mrs. Harris didn't have any problem getting us to listen and we asked a zillion questions like, how far away those countries were and how far airplanes could fly. None of us could understand why the Axis countries were bombing our Allies and the U.S. territories and killing so many soldiers and sailors. No one in the class had ever seen a Japanese person and we knew almost nothing about Japan. However, almost everyone in the class knew what Germans and Italians looked like, for many of us were from German families and some of the kids had Italian families.

Tuck made a visit to see us and said that he was unhappy with the situation at the Harrises (not my teacher, but Dorothy's sisters), who were taking care of his son, Herbie. He believed that they were trying to adopt Herbie. Mom didn't want any part of the adoption process. She said to Tuck, "If they are going to change Herbie's name from Shipe to Harris, then bring Herbie here and I will raise him for you."

Tuck told Mom that all or any of the furniture that remained in his house in Springfield could be moved here if we could get someone to help us move it. Tuck had an Aladdin lamp with him from his house and gave it to Mom. It had a carbon mantle that gave enough light that we could read a book across the room from it. We were warned how fragile and expensive the mantles were.

Within a month, Tuck and Lena had gone to the Harrises' home and picked up Herbie and brought him to the mountain. They learned that the Harrises were, indeed, filing for adoption. Herbie slept with Mom and Georgia. Dad, Jesse and I continued to sleep in one bed. Herbie wasn't much of a problem except for one thing: He loved his grandfather and when Dad would go out the door without closing it tight, Herbie would be right behind him, heading for the barn or fields.

The family had a good Easter. Lena and Betty came with their husbands, Robert Lee and Buss. I got a nice Easter basket that was wrapped with a beautiful green cellophane wrap. Inside the basket was the largest chocolate rabbit I had ever seen. I wanted to keep the rabbit as long as possible. I did eat some of the tail and the bottom of the feet, enough to determine that he was hollow.

During dinner Buss and Betty were talking about going to Baltimore and getting jobs at the Glen L. Martin Aircraft Company in Middle River near Essex, Maryland. Robert Lee and Lena talked about the fact that if Robert Lee volunteered for the Army Air Force it might be possible that Robert Lee would be sent to Chenault Field near Chicago as an aircraft engine instructor because of his experience as a head mechanic at the Chevrolet garage in Romney.

Herbie with Cookie at home on Martins Mountain—1942

When it became dark, Dad asked everyone to come out on the porch, and he pointed out that the red glow in the sky was due to a fire on Warrior Mountain. We saw the flames rise into the air as the fire burned large evergreen trees. Dad believed that if the wind didn't shift that it would be little concern to our mountain. The fire was in an isolated part of Warrior Mountain with little danger to houses.

Early the next morning Mr. Condy Miller from the Consolidated Orchard Company came by the house and asked Dad if he would join volunteers to take preventative actions to keep the fire on Warrior Mountain from spreading to Martins Mountain and damaging the orchard or any of the equipment. The fire spreading to Martins Mountain was now a possibility for the wind was blowing toward us. Mom packed Dad a sack lunch and he climbed on the truck with the crew and they were off heading toward the orchard.

Jesse and I were both home during Easter vacation from school; Georgia was spending a couple days with a girl friend. About noon we could smell smoke and noticed that the fire on Warrior Mountain was much closer and could possibly be on Walnut Ridge, a small ridge running between Warrior and Martins Mountain on the east side of our house. Mom told us not to worry, for the firefighters would come and warn us if anything about the fire became a danger to us.

The wind began to blow much harder. It was blowing so hard that it sounded like a gale on a cold winter night that causes the power lines to sing a ghostly sound, a sound that sends shivers up and down your spine. We sensed that our situation was changing for the worst, but we didn't say anything about being scared.

More smoke was bellowing overhead. The sun was an amber color and it made the skin on our faces appear bronze. It was difficult to determine which direction the smoke was coming from. Jesse ran up the road about a half-mile for he thought that the fire was now on Martins Mountain. He ran back and said that it was hard to determine, but he believed that we had fire coming up both sides of our mountain and coming toward us—we might be trapped.

Mom determined that we shouldn't make a run for it, and that since we had some protection from the plowed fields and grass fields on both sides of the house we stood a good chance of fighting the fire to keep it away from the buildings. She decided we would stay put and she assured us that she believed the firefighters would come and help us, and they would have trucks to haul us from harm's way if we had to leave the mountain.

The situation worsened. Jesse took control, sending Mom and me to various buildings to determine if any were burning or in danger of catching on fire from the flying embers. He sent me to check the mule shed, the spray shed and the cow shed while he checked the hay shed. Mom checked in the house where Herbie was and she checked the chicken house. Mom made sure Herbie would stay put in the house and that he had something to keep him busy.

Jesse came running from the hay shed and yelled, "Grab buckets of water, the hay shed is on fire!" Mom and I grabbed four of the hog-watering buckets and filled them at the pump with five gallons each. We ran to the hay shed. Both of us had spilled half the water we started with and by the time we got there, Jesse had dragged some burning burlap bags from the building. He used the water to wet the bags and then he wet down the floor in the shed where the bags had laid.

I was gasping for breath and my throat felt like it was on fire and I saw that Mom and Jesse were also gasping for air. The wind was swirling around us, picking up leaves and paper and carrying them into the air and mixing them with the embers. The sky was almost dark except for swirling embers; at times they were like fireworks in the dark noonday sky.

By the time we got back to the yard at the house we had to lie down to catch a breath of air; things had gone beyond our control. We turned the hogs loose and they ran into the field and huddled together in a tight bunch.

There was fire on the east and west sides of our mountain; it had reached the road on the west side across from the house and the pigpens were on fire. Fire was racing up trees. It would climb the vines in the trees, and cedar and pine trees would explode in huge showers of sparks and embers. It was like a cyclone boring into the sky and we could feel the heat increase.

We decided not to release the chickens. We believed the chickens didn't have good sense and they would likely fly into the fire instead of away from it.

Mom instructed me to gather what clothes I could carry from the bedroom closets and throw them on the ground and cover them with a tarpaulin. It appeared to her that with so many embers flying around, the only thing keeping the house from burning was the metal roof. I grabbed my chocolate rabbit as I was leaving the living room and placed it in my American Flyer wagon and pulled the wagon outdoors. Queenie and her pup Butch, our outside dogs, and Cookie, our inside dog, were scared plenty; they stuck close with us.

Mom said, "Let's all lay here together on the ground. Keep an eye out for live embers that might fall on our clothes." She fashioned wet cloths for our noses. Herbie wouldn't hold the cloth over his nose so Mom ripped one of the rags into a small strip and tied the wet cloth on his face.

Our condition was desperate. Mom began praying to God to deliver us from the clutches of the firestorm.

About an hour or so we heard the sound of raindrops hitting the canvas that covered the clothes—huge drops that come first during a rainstorm and make a loud splat sound. Soon the wind shifted and the air began to cool and in about an hour we could sit up and take a few good deep breaths of air. The rain began to knock down the flames and the wind was carrying the smoke away from our part of the mountain.

We went into the house, slumped in chairs at the kitchen table and drank water to cool our parched throats. After a bit, we began pointing out to each other how our faces were black from the soot and our clothes were a mess. Mom said that we looked like raccoons for we had sooty black faces and had rubbed our eyes so much that the tears caused from the smoke had washed circles around our eyes.

About eleven that night Dad got off the truck at the road and when he came into the house Mom was really on him for not coming to help us. Dad told us that the firefighters didn't know that the fire had gotten around them like it had and that we were in such grave danger, for the crews were at the north end of the Consolidated Orchard Company property, about four miles away. They were using bulldozers to dig firebreaks.

We took flashlights and lanterns and made sure that the animals were safe in their areas. Dad strung some woven wire and fixed a temporary place for the hogs, and we took feed and water to all of the animals. We could see that some trees and stumps continued to burn. Dad said that the smoke and terrible smell would be with us for days and maybe weeks.

I shined the flashlight into the bed of my wagon and saw that the chocolate rabbit had melted into a heap. I got a butcher knife from the kitchen and scraped the remains into a bowl, for no forest fire was going to deny me the joy of eating the biggest Easter rabbit I had ever seen in all my born days.

Fire crews were on the job early the next morning. They used backpack water sprayers to douse the stumps and hot spots. Firefighters returned for a couple of days and then declared the mountain safe. It took us weeks before we felt safe to go to bed without someone checking outside for any signs of fire.

The forest fire warden told Dad and Mom that they had not been able to predict the track of the fire once the fire overran the fire tower on Warrior Mountain. Without the ability to get up high, they couldn't determine the full extent of the danger. The warden explained that when the winds became so strong the fire swept along the east side of Martins Mountain and then the embers were blown up and over to the west side. If the rain hadn't come when the cold front moved through and shifted the wind then the fire would have burned to the Millstone store and perhaps to the North Branch of the Potomac River.

The decision to stay on the mountain was not a good one and the lives of all the people on Martins Mountain and the hollows on both sides had been in grave danger.

Mom never commented on the fire warden's remarks or why she thought the rain came when the firefighters didn't. I knew why—I remember her praying for God to save her family in the flood in West Virginia and He honored her prayer and now He had honored her prayer again. I noticed that Mom's nagging cough continued.

Mr. Millholland came to the house and he seemed in better spirits than usual, even though the fire could have destroyed his property. He told Dad that the county agents were predicting great opportunities for farmers during wartime. He said that the agents believed that if sharecroppers were ever going to make good, it would be now. The agents predicted that every crop that could be harvested could easily be sold and at record-high prices unless the government established price controls.

Mr. Millholland said to Dad, "Based on what the agents were saying, we should plant every square inch of land that is cleared, and clear additional land." All of us listening had smiles on our faces except for Dad.

When Mr. Millholland left Dad said, "We can't take on any more work. All of us are working as hard as we can, and I am working from before daylight to well after dark."

Dad worked out a new plan for what and how much he would plant. He also began looking into equipment that would lessen his burden. He priced some tractors and was asking around how much having a tractor could help. A man brought a tractor to our place for Dad to try out. This was the most unusual thing any of us had ever seen. It used a Model "A" Ford car frame and engine and it had large steel rear wheels with cleats. The wheels had a gear that went around the outer edge of the wheel and it was turned by a gear where the car's rear wheel normally would be. This strange contraption moved very slowly and Dad said it would have a lot of power and that it had promise to meet our needs. The tractor was made from a kit purchased from Sears, Roebuck & Company

One of the major reasons that farmers working mountain terrain seldom used tractors was that the tractors would easily roll over, and often when the tractor was pulling straight up a hill it would rise up in the front and turn over on top of the driver. Most of the local men that came by to see the tractor believed that the wide front and rear wheels would help keep this tractor from being too dangerous. Dad bought the tractor.

Another contraption that Dad purchased to reduce his burden was a crosscut sawmill. Dad paid thirty dollars for the rig, a Model "T" Ford car frame with the body and wheels removed. A wide pulley was attached to one of the rear wheel drums and a heavy woven cloth belt was attached to a sawmill pulley. The sawmill had a large circular blade without any cover or protection for the operator.

Dad ran the saw. Jesse carried the logs and tree limbs to Dad from a stack that we had earlier dragged to the saw area by mule team. I had the job of grabbing the cut-off blocks of firewood and stacking them.

The sawmill did shorten the time it took to cut our firewood, but it was very dangerous. Mom hated to see us sawing firewood. She complained about the pieces flying around and how we could be hit in the eyes and how the saw would kick out some pieces and they would fly every which way. The contraption was just another thing that Mom would pray over for our safety.

I saw an ad in the *Progressive Farmer* magazine offering boys an opportunity to sell and deliver *GRIT* newspapers. This was a weekly newspaper that was sent through the mail to the newsboys and all you needed to get started was ten customers. I canvassed the people on the mountain and came up with ten. My papers arrived and I also received my first gift, a *GRIT* newspaper delivery bag. I slung the strap over my shoulder and headed out walking to deliver newspapers to my customers, who were mostly grouped together at the orchard camp and the bunkhouse. I felt real good about being in business and as I dreamed about my success the papers weren't heavy and the four miles didn't seem far at all. Each paper sold for a dime and I could keep three cents per copy. I paid the postage for the weekly order, and after my expenses of postage and a money order, my profit was twenty-seven cents per week.

I also found in a magazine that I could send off for chance cards and by selling the chances I could make money or win valuable prizes. Each card had a value of ten dollars after all forty chances were sold. The winner could win a bed comforter or a Swiss weather predictor and for my effort, I could choose one of the prizes or keep five bucks. The weather predictor hung on the wall and if it were going to be sunny, a little Swiss maid appeared, and if it were going to rain, a little Swiss boy carrying an umbrella would appear. The chances sold like hot cakes, especially at the bunkhouse on the orchard for the bachelor men loved to gamble.

My newspaper business couldn't grow unless I went off the mountain to where more customers lived but the chance card sales were going great. It wasn't long until I was able to give Mom a new comforter made of a material that had large roses on it. A month later I was able to hang a weather predictor in Mom's kitchen. She really liked it and told me she looked at it morning and afternoon and it was right for weather predictions most of the time.

The bunkhouse guys were crazy about taking chances to win. The chances were lifted from the board using the tip of a penknife. Many of the guys made their choices from what they thought were lucky names like Sue, Jan, Jill, etc. It wasn't only the bunkhouse guys, but also, the housewives at the orchard who wanted in on the hot action, some housewives would take ten punches that cost them a whole two and a half bucks.

I always went to the bunkhouse after quitting time to make sure a large number of guys were around when I removed the seal that revealed the grand prize winner. When I announced the winner, the losers would cuss and swear that they weren't going to take any more chances. I always had a new card with me and when one guy would take a chance it was like chumming the water with bait to attract fish, they stood in line to make sure they got a chance to win.

I learned early on that hardly any of the men in the bunkhouse could read or write, for they always asked me to write their name on the back of the card by the appropriate three-letter name that matched their chance selection. I decided early on that I would never cheat these guys, and I believed they trusted me, for I was sure they couldn't remember which names that were on the chances they had chosen. I also decided never to discuss with anyone the number of chances a housewife took.

Every opportunity I had, when Mom and Dad were together, I showed them the magazine picture of a boy on a bicycle with his *GRIT* newspaper bag over his shoulder and I told them how good I would look delivering my papers on a bike.

After selling my third chance card I chose a comforter for one of my prizes instead of keeping the money. When the comforter arrived by mail I put it on our bed and showed Dad how nice it looked and told him how warm we would be under it. I also slipped in a plug for how the bike would take less time on my route and that the days were getting shorter as winter approached and I would have less time between finishing my chores and delivering the papers before dark.

The day arrived! Mom and Dad were taking me to Montgomery Ward's in Cumberland to get my bike, for they had the one I wanted on sale. My bike was a beautiful green and white model with coaster brakes and a tank compartment where batteries for a horn and light were stored. Jesse made the comment that I was the first kid in the family to own a bike. I could already ride a bike because my friends, Bill Reckley and Gladstone Beeler, had bikes and they had taught me to ride.

Kenneth Cage, my buddy from school, was invited to come home with me on a weekend. He didn't mind helping me rush to finish my chores, so that we could play. We had a great time. Kenneth loved to ride the mules and we would ride bare-backed for so long that when we jumped off, our feet would be numb and we could hardly walk.

We set up tin can and glass bottle targets and shot at them with .22 rifles. We had plenty of ammunition. Dad and Tuck would empty their pockets of ammunition into a drawer next to the corner in the kitchen. Dad had double-barreled and single-barreled 12-gauge shotguns, and he stood them in the corner of the kitchen. We didn't mess with the shotguns much for they kicked, and after a bit we would have red shoulders and often a bruised cheek.

On a particular Saturday after Kenneth and I finished the chores, we put in for Mom to give us permission to ride the bicycle down the mountain to the Millstone. We promised to be home by supper. Mom said we could, so off we went riding double, Kenneth riding sideways on the bar in front of me. We both had experience riding on the sandy dirt roads and we knew to pay particular attention to steer clear of deep sandy spots, for it was nearly impossible to steer a bike in them.

We were doing great and I didn't have to pedal at all as we passed the high-power electric lines. I knew from there on it would be steeper and steeper grades for over a mile and a half. We made it through the "S" curves where the worst sandy spots were. I smelled something like oil burning and realized the brakes were hot. We rounded the sharp curve at the big white oak tree and headed for the straightaway and the steepest section of road on the mountain. I was standing up on the pedals and applying brakes as hard as I could. Then something made a loud "snap" and the pedals began to spin. The coaster brakes failed and my rotating knees knocked Kenneth off the bar and we were both now sliding down the road on our feet struggling to hold the bike upright. We were yelling instructions and none made any sense, for we realized that we couldn't continue holding the bike upright and we were doomed to crash! The gravel in the road was ripping our shoe soles and heels off. The pedals continued to spin and were pounding the back of my legs. Stopping the bike was hopeless. A curve was coming up and in our struggle to maintain our balance, I had only one choice and that was to steer the bike into a drainage ditch. At the end of the ditch we went out into the brush and eventually tumbled over each other and stopped in a heap, just before hitting a huge boulder.

We were scratched and bruised badly and had some bleeding cuts on our knees, elbows and our heads. Our clothes were ripped and our shoe heels were gone and the soles were nearly worn through. We sat on the ground for a while. The brake drum had turned blue from the heat and continued to smoke.

We didn't have any way to take care of our wounds. Our brush burns were stinging like crazy and we were trembling from the fright of what we had gone through. We left the bike in the woods and limped back home.

Mom washed our wounds with Octagon soap. She said that the soap would kill the germs; it burned real bad. The iodine was worse. Kenneth danced around yelling, "Stop Pearlzie, you're set'n me on fire. No more, the rest of my wounds will heal on their own." He called her Pearlzie instead of Mrs. Shipe; Mom preferred the nickname better than him calling her Pearl. Mom continued dabbing us with iodine each time we stopped dancing and yelling. A bloody water fluid was oozing from our wounds.

Dad and Jesse came in from the field and after we told them what happened, Dad said, "You boys probably were going thirty-five to forty miles an hour and you're lucky you didn't kill yourselves or break your necks. Don't ever ride double down the mountain again. Bike brakes can't handle the load." Jesse took the truck and brought the bike home. We men inspected it and as suspected the New Departure coaster brake discs had become so hot that they expanded and welded together, which caused the brake arm to break, and that was the reason the pedals were going around. The bike had spokes missing, the wheel rims were bent, and the fenders were torn loose from the brackets.

I didn't approach Mom and Dad for money to fix my bike. I looked up the price of new parts in the catalogue and to my surprise the parts would cost nearly as much as a new bike. Walking became my way of getting around and taking care of my businesses. Doing business wasn't as much fun any more.

The Farm Bureau agents were correct: We not only could sell all the vegetables we grew, but people were coming to our place to purchase vegetables from the fields. Our cantaloupes and watermelons were especially sought after and we had a bumper crop of them. As the word got around, customers were coming to purchase our vegetables by the truckload.

The few apples that we had were not the best. Most had hail damage, some had brown spots on them, and they were wormy. Mr. Millholland had found a market for our apples to be used for juice. We picked them and loaded them into boxcars that were on a siding behind the A&P market in Cumberland. We dumped the apples loose into the railroad cars, placing boards in the doorway, one above the other until we filled the car to within 18 inches of the top. An inspector came and verified that we had filled the car and shut the door and applied a metal band with a lead seal. He squeezed the lead seal with a pair of pliers that imprinted his number on the seal.

The sixth grade started with a surprise for me and six other kids: during the first week of school we were notified that we would be promoted to the seventh grade. At first I was happy because I wouldn't have Mrs. Thomas as a teacher. She didn't put up with any cutting up in her class and everyone said she was the toughest math teacher that they had ever had. But on the other hand, I wasn't happy about leaving my classmates, whom I had been with since the second grade. Mom was very proud of me and that sealed the deal. I was now in junior high school, and began doing things like changing classes each period and having study hall.

I ran slam into algebra I and for the first time in all my born days I couldn't figure out what it was all about. I read the book and did the examples, but it just wasn't coming through. If it hadn't been for my classmate Ida Mae Crane, who was a whiz at everything, smarter than any of us kids and good looking too, I would have failed my first subject in school.

One of the first opportunities that I had to help out in the war effort was to respond to a notice at school which asked everyone to collect ripe milkweed pods, put them into burlap bags, and deliver them to the Oldtown School. The silky fibers from the pods would be used as filler in life preservers. I gathered ten bags full of the pods and imagined that the fibers from my collection effort would save the life of one of our fighting men.

Our country was losing a lot of men. The *Cumberland Evening Times* listed the servicemen killed, wounded or missing in action and some days there were two columns of names. Some of our neighbors who had men in the service had a small flag with a blue star for each serviceman. Some homes had a gold star, which meant that one of their loved ones had been killed.

We were preparing to butcher five hogs and Dad had three neighbor men in to help us. We had cut long poles and fashioned them into three-legged lifts to hang the hog's upright. We used our large sled for a platform. We filled a fifty-gallon drum mounted at one end of the platform with water and built a roaring fire beneath it to bring the water to a boil. We dragged the hog carcasses back and forth in the drum to scald the skin and loosen the hair, and then used scrapers to shave the hair and scruff off. Dad added wood ashes to the water, which helped remove the scruff. When finished, the carcass would be as clean as a man's freshly shaved face.

Dad always used a .22 caliber rifle to kill the hogs. When the crew was ready to take the first hog he handed me the rifle, and my heart went into my throat. The men knew it was my first time to kill a hog, so they stood along the fence to watch. They reminded me that they had a jar ready to capture the squeal if I missed. I had heard this at other butchering times and now it was my turn to perform under the watchful eye of a group of men. I remembered stories of hog skulls left honeycombed because a .22 caliber long bullet wouldn't penetrate; and hogs that jerked at the moment the trigger was pulled, causing the shooter to miss. I realized how important it was for me to be completely focused on what I had to do. The danger to Dad was great, because he was down in the pen standing near the hog. If I missed and only inflicted a wound, the hog could turn on him. Using its tusks, it could rip Dad's legs apart. Dad had a very sharp knife in his hand ready to slit the jugular vein in the hog's throat as soon as the animal went down.

My rite of passage to a higher level on the journey to manhood was now in my own hands. I raised the rifle, a calm came over me and my hands quit shaking. I had an assurance within that I could do this task. I aimed as I had been instructed, sighting on the point where the imaginary lines from each ear to the opposite eye crossed, and squeezed the trigger. The rifle fired, the hog went down thud, and Dad did his job flawlessly.

As was his custom, Dad didn't say a word about my feat. He handed me the rifle four more times that day as the butchering continued. It was nearly dark by the time the five carcasses were gutted and hung to cool.

Early the next morning we were all cutting meat, Dad doing the fine detailed trimming of the hams and shoulders, trimming each one for the sugar-curing process. Mom was stripping out the tenderloins and cutting them to fit in wide-mouthed canning jars. Jesse was cutting and trimming the backbone, ribs and bacon sides. I was cutting the fat into small cubes for rendering into lard. We threw the lean cuts into a tub for grinding into sausage. We worked all day and into the night. I was the first to be told to get cleaned up and hit the sack because I was becoming careless with the very sharp knives.

Mom was up early and had fresh sausage frying, with eggs and homemade biscuits. We all ate a hardy breakfast and began the third day of butchering. I built fires under the two black iron pots and started rendering the fat chunks into grease for making lard. Mom and Jesse were cleaning the intestines for use as casings for sausage. We took turns turning the grinder until we had ground a No.10 washtub full of sausage.

When the fat had boiled to the point that the chunks began to float, Dad verified that it was time to start putting the fat into the lard press. The press squeezed the grease out of the chunks, leaving a cake of cracklings. We all picked at the cake and ate the hot cracklings and pork rinds.

As soon as the fat rendering was complete and the crocks of grease were taken to the cellar to cool into lard, I added water to the iron pots and began bringing the water to a boil. Mom began putting the hogs' heads and other parts into the pots for cooking the meat off the bones. The broth and meat were used to make souse and cornpone and the stock was canned for seasoning of other pork dishes.

We cooked and ate some of the tongue, ears and feet. We loved sauerkraut and pigs' feet and we loved, in particular, brains mixed in fried eggs. Most people gag when they hear that we ate this, but we loved it. We didn't waste any parts of the hog. We even hung the lungs in the coop for the chickens to pick at, and our dogs and cats ate scraps until they almost burst. We carried the entrails into the woods and made piles for the wild animals to eat.

Dad prepared the salt brine for curing the hams and shoulders. He placed a fresh egg in water and added salt until the egg floated to within three inches of the surface, then lowered the meat into the barrels and placed boards on top. He used a large rock to hold down the boards so that the meat would remain submerged.

I asked, "Where did you learn to do that, to use a fresh egg to determine the amount of salt to add?"

He said, "My dad did it that way."

We made the last trip from Tuck's house, bringing furniture and other valuable things. Tuck and Dorothy had a new refrigerator that had never been removed from its carton, and Dad brought it to the house even though we didn't have electricity. (The house did have one electric wire, which was connected to any empty socket that hung from the ceiling in the living room. I used the beaded chain that hung from the socket as a way to measure my growth; I could touch the end of the chain by stretching my arm over my head.)

The war was putting a damper on everything and the government was establishing price controls and rationing. Dad received a "T" gasoline rationing sticker for his truck and that allowed us to have enough gasoline to operate the truck almost as we did before rationing. Most people had an "A" sticker for their cars and were forced to car-pool just to get to work. Sometimes when family and friends were at our house and were afraid that they might run out of gasoline before they got home, Dad would use a hose and siphon gasoline from his truck and give them enough to get home.

Christmas and New Year's came and went. The news from the war fronts was terrible. It was impossible for my family to celebrate as before because of the suffering the Axis forces caused for the Allied forces and countries.

Lena's husband, Robert Lee, was not home for Christmas; he was at Chenault Field in Illinois. Georgia had quit school and taken a job at a defense plant in Baltimore. Betty and her husband Buss made it home for the holidays from their jobs at the Glen L. Martin Company plant in Essex, Maryland. Jesse had turned sixteen in November and Bill was now twenty-five. Mom knew that the war was coming closer and closer to her family. We didn't talk about it.

9

Brothers drafted for WWII

We had some good snow the weekend Kenneth Cage came to visit. We hunted rabbits by tracking them in the snow and were able to shoot a few. I skinned them and Mom fried them up for dinner, dipping the meat in flour and frying the rabbit the way she fried chicken. The rabbits were nice and plump and to Kenneth and me, tasted better than chicken.

After dinner we asked Mom if we could ride my new sled down the mountain road to the Millstone store, and we assured her that we would be back before supper. She inquired about how we would be able to control the speed of the sled and not wear out the toes of our shoes as we steered with our feet. We showed her that we had a braking system that wouldn't fail: We had fastened pieces from a set of tire chains to the front of the sled, so that if the sled began going too fast we would simply allow the chains to drop in front of both runners, which would create enough drag to bring us to a stop. We demonstrated the chain brakes to Mom out in the front yard and then she gave us permission to go to the store. She also reached into her bra, pulled out her handkerchief that had some change tied in one corner and gave each of us a dime. This was her private bank, where she kept the money she made from the sale of chicken eggs.

We knew the mountain road well. Cars and trucks had pounded the snow into a hard mass of tire tracks. Kenneth was on my back. His job was to watch for oncoming cars and trucks because the snowbanks beside the road were too high for me see over. We passed the high power lines and were doing great. My new sled handled well. The biggest problem was my eyes watering from the icy wind. Every now and then Kenneth would really squeeze me hard as we zipped through the curves.

We approached some "S" turns where the road wound through a series of rock outcroppings and began to hit spots where the snow had melted from the sun and then frozen again into glare ice. Our speed kept increasing and we were going faster than I had ever ridden a sled. Kenneth began to scream and he yelled at me to put on the brakes. I dropped both chains and they dug into the ice. Then there was a jerk on both handles of the sled as the chains ripped off. The brakes didn't work! We were doomed to crash!

Kenneth screamed, "Do something!"

We had been dragging our toes but it hadn't helped. I tried to steer through the turns but couldn't, and we began to fishtail, out of control. Then we overturned. Over and over we went on the icy road until we slammed against some rock ledges and stopped abruptly.

Sitting up, we began taking inventory. We were a mess. We had scratches on our faces and hands, I had a painful hip bruise and Kenneth was complaining about his arms and elbows. We had worn down the toes of our shoes and ripped the knees out of our pants. My good school coat was torn at the elbows and my gloves were shredded.

I looked at my sled. It was tilted to one side. Maybe, I thought, the tilt was due to one runner being in deeper snow. Then I saw that all the runner supports on one side were bent flat to the bottom and the runner was bent in a U shape.

Kenneth wanted to head home right away. I couldn't figure why he was so anxious about hurrying home for there wasn't going to be any joy in telling Mom and Dad about our accident. As I began to brush off my pant legs the answer became obvious to me: The back of my legs were wet and my pants were frozen stiff, and I realized that Kenneth had wet his pants. I began to laugh and he made me swear to never tell anyone and I promised I wouldn't. I couldn't stop laughing about Kenneth wetting his pants, but I wasn't going to have any fun from it for I swore to secrecy.

I really wanted to cry, for now the mountain had claimed not only my new bicycle but also my new sled.

Dad was sitting at the shoe last and repairing the toes of our shoes. He growled, "You boys should have better sense than to believe that you could ride a sled double and be able to stop on this steep road. When in the hell are you going to learn your lesson about getting off the mountain? Maybe you should think about walking!"

We didn't mention that the failed braking system, my ruined sled, or the condition of our school clothes. We stayed clear of Dad, doing all of our regular chores plus extra work too. We made sure all of the animal troughs had the ice broken and water added. We even split extra wood and kindling and carried plenty of it to the wood boxes behind both stoves and filled the box on the porch.

We had our fingers crossed that Dad wouldn't notice how Mom was sewing patches on our good clothes, especially my new school coat.

It was a very cold February day. Dad had gone to the Post Office and brought home the mail and evening paper and laid them on the living room table. After supper Mom was looking through the mail and found a letter from her brother Bill and his wife Katie, who lived in Bedford, Pennsylvania. As Mom began to read the letter she gasped and said, "Lord have Mercy!"

Dad looked from his paper and asked, "What happened?"

Mom began to read aloud: "Dear Pearl and Russ, We hate to get the news to you this way, but since you don't have a telephone we thought this letter would be better than someone from the orchard taking our call and delivering the message.

"Army Air Force officers came last week and informed us that our Billy had been killed in a B-24 bomber crash in the jungles of Brazil. The bomber squadron was flying to North Africa when it crashed. The officers thought his body would be delivered to Bedford in about a month. We will let you know when the military funeral will be scheduled. We will bury him here in Bedford."

Mom sobbed and then said, "This war is going to kill all of our young boys and there's not a thing we can do except keep sending them to their death."

One morning, Dad said to Kenneth and me at the breakfast table, "I want you boys to get a rope halter on Little Jersey and take her down to Columbus Delauder's place and get her serviced."

We both looked at each other and I answered, "Okay, but I have never been to his house."

Dad said, "Lead Little Jersey down the road and at the power lines take the path down the side of the mountain to the road that runs along our mountain. Stay on it and at the fork that goes up on Walnut ridge, stay left. Columbus lives at the end of the road in that hollow. It will take you about two hours to walk it. You stay there until she's serviced, then lead her back, Okay?"

I answered, "Okay."

I noticed that Mom was rolling her eyes in disgust at Dad talking about such a subject at her breakfast table.

Kenneth and I went directly to the cowshed and put a rope halter on Little Jersey and led her out through the gate. Grannie and Nellie, the other cows, started to bawl and bellow. Little Jersey returned their calls and when we began to get out of sight of the other cows she started to pullback on the rope lead. Kenneth broke off a small sapling and stripped it into a switch and whacked Little Jersey a few times on her butt and she began to follow without my pulling on the lead.

The path down the high power lines zigzagged off the mountain and when we reached the rock outcroppings and cliffs Little Jersey balked at almost every turn because she almost had to sit down on her hind legs to keep from sliding out of control.

It was a beautiful sunny day and we finally reached Columbus Delauder's house, which was the only house up in Frog Hollow. His kids came out to meet us and asked, "What are you doing with your cow?"

I didn't answer but instead asked, "Is your Dad here?"

They answered, "Yea, he's at the barn."

I said, "Well that's where we need to take Little Jersey."

Once there, Columbus took Little Jersey and put her in the corral with his bull.

Kenneth whispered to me, "I had this service thing all figured out before we got here. How about you?"

I replied, "I'd be lying if I said I had it figured out."

Neither Kenneth nor I had ever seen anything like this! We wanted to laugh, but with Columbus being our Sunday school teacher, we knew better. I said to Kenneth, "The whole purpose is that Little Jersey will have a calf and then be 'fresh' and provide milk for our family. Then we will quit milking one of the other cows and it will become 'dry' and then it will be that cow's turn to get serviced. If everything works out we will have milk, butter, schmierkase and buttermilk all year long."

We watched the two animals mate. Then we went with Columbus. He showed us the pump house and spring, which was the water source for the whole Consolidated Orchard Company. He handed us a large tin dipper and we drank of the fresh springwater. It tasted really good and was cold without having to put ice in it.

Columbus handed me Little Jersey's lead and Kenneth and I began leading her back down the road. Little Jersey appeared ready to go home. The sun continued shinning and we were enjoying the walk.

Suddenly Kenneth yelled, "Oh my God, here comes the bull!"

I said, "Don't worry there's a fence between us."

The bull hit the fence and it didn't slow him at all. He broke the two strands of barbed wire and was coming toward us with the wire and two fence posts dangling from his horns.

"He's going to kill us!" Kenneth yelled. He ran ahead and climbed up an apple tree. I decided that the tree would hold both of us and Little Jersey could handle the situation, so I ran and joined Kenneth in the tree.

Columbus was running down the road with his bull cinch pole, which had a hook on the end that could be snapped into the ring that was in the bull's nose. Using the pole, Columbus could control the bull.

From the apple tree we had a great seat to watch Little Jersey get serviced again, but this time she and the bull were entangled in barbed wire and fence posts. Columbus was yelling, "Come back here you dumb bastard!" But he waited for the servicing to end and then hooked the bull's nose ring and held the animal steady. Columbus said, "Okay, boys, you can continue taking your heifer home."

We looked back and saw that Columbus had control of the bull but the bull continued to pawl dirt with his front hooves and was throwing dust high in the air. We could hear Columbus yelling, "Damn you bull, if you aren't careful I'll castrate you and then you won't behave like this anymore."

As we climbed the steep path on the power line we stopped two or three times and at each pause we reviewed the experience. I said to Kenneth, "What a chicken! You climbed that tree like a squirrel and you must have been fifteen feet up there."

Kenneth replied, "I noticed who had a perch just below me. And just who is the biggest chicken?"

I wanted to tell Dad the outrageous story about taking Little Jersey to get her serviced, but I couldn't bring myself to even mention how we had been enlightened beyond our wildest imagination. Columbus let Kenneth and me know that he had told Dad about the episode. Dad never mentioned it to us boys.

I had only been to two funerals. One was Bess Lookabaugh's. She was the lady who helped raise Mom's sister, Aunt Boots. She was elderly and loved by her family and friends, many of whom knew that she was about to die and were expecting it. The other was Dorothy's funeral. I knew that going to Billy's funeral was going to be different because it would be a military funeral and Billy was young and handsome and his family was large and very close. He had been a machine-gunner in the belly turret of a B-24 Liberator bomber and had recently been promoted to sergeant.

We arrived at the church in Bedford to attend the funeral of my cousin, Sgt. William S. Shipe. A group of soldiers carried Billy's flag-draped, silver casket into the crowded church. We Shipes sat in the back. Most of the family, Mom's side, was there. I kept my head bowed for I was concerned that I might make eye contact with my cousins and I didn't know how to act, for I sensed that they were very sad and hurting inside, like I was, but probably a hundred times more.

At Billy's grave I believed that I was doing okay, no tears, even though almost everyone was crying. The honor guard fired three rounds into the air, and at each shot people jerked and the sharp sounds mixed with sobs from the mourners. A bugler standing off in the distance began playing *Retreat* and the sounds ripped through my heart. Hate for the enemy that had killed Billy rose up within me. I burst into tears and couldn't hold them back. My chest was heaving. I ran from the grave and jumped in Tuck's car. I was so angry. If ever any Nazis or Japs had crossed my path I could easily have killed them.

Our family and others went back to Uncle Bill's and Aunt Katie's house.

Uncle Bill sobbed as he told about how hurt he and Aunt Katie were when they opened the box of Billy's personal things that the Army sent to them. The box contained a bloodstained flight suit and broken goggles. Uncle Bill sobbed as he told the story. I left the room. Only a few people were able to stay. Mom sat with her brother and in time he was doing better.

Some food was served, but I couldn't eat and I felt bad about not knowing what to say to my cousins. I went out and sat in the car. I felt so empty. I now knew what this war was doing to families and how much pain the deaths of so many servicemen was causing.

Mr. Millholland and Dad were putting their heads together to determine the impact of the war on our truck gardening and whether it would be best to grow fewer garden vegetables and more feed grains. The Government was pushing everyone that had any land to plant a Victory Garden. The strict rationing of gasoline and tires and food was making it difficult for us to get the produce to market and only a few people were able to travel to the mountain to purchase produce. Garden vegetables required about twice the work of field crops and Dad wasn't able to get help. The mountain road was hard on the wartime synthetic tires, so often my brother Tuck would park his car at the Millstone and walk up the mountain to save wear and tear on his tires. Usually, any one walking the road would be picked up and given a lift.

My sister Betty and her husband Buss came home for the fourth of July and worked a deal with Mom and Dad that I could go to their place in Essex, Maryland for one week. Soon the time came for us to leave. I was determined to stay awake all the way and see all the sights, but I fell asleep during the five-hour trip and woke up when we arrived in Essex.

Betty and Buss lived in a small house trailer that had only had one bed and a tiny kitchen and a place for two to sit at a table. I slept on a small couch. The trailer was located next to the Pennsylvania Railroad lines between Baltimore and New York. Electric trains seemed to pass about every 30 minutes or less, traveling at about 60 miles per hour through that area. Slower freight trains were loaded with tanks, trucks, cannons and canvas-covered war supplies. Military armed guards were riding on the open cars.

One day we were driving along a road and it appeared to me that we were in the countryside. But just as I was about to remark to Betty about how unusual the countryside looked, we drove under some netting. The countryside I was looking at was really the camouflaged Glen L. Martin factory and adjoining parking lots. Buss said the roofs of the factory buildings also were camouflaged to match the parking lot netting and the runways were painted so that they matched too. "From the air this place looks like three or four farms with corn and hay fields."

On another afternoon Buss arrived home from work and all excited about a Glen L. Martin-built four-engine flying boat that had crashed in the water near Middle River Point. He grabbed a piece of hose and siphoned some gasoline from his car and put it into the gas tank on his speedboat and within minutes we were approaching a PBM-1 Mars flying boat. The airplane was listing badly, the left wingtip was in the water, and the hull was wrinkled and cracked. A number of boats surrounded the plane.

Buss throttled back as a fast-approaching boat headed our way with a siren shrieking and a uniformed officer yelling over a megaphone for Buss to stop. The boat came alongside and the officer announced that we were in a restricted area and we had to leave immediately. The officer told Buss to turn over his camera and film, then opened the camera and pulled the film out and dropped it into his boat.

The officer then questioned Buss about where he got the gasoline for pleasure-riding. Buss told him that he had siphoned it from his car. The officer gave Buss a citation and said that he would be reported to his rationing board for misuse of gasoline. Then the officer directed us to leave the area immediately and instructed us not to discuss what we had seen without government approval. The patrol boat escorted us back to the dock at Middle River.

I spent my days reading comic books while Betty and Buss were at work. One day I noticed a piggy bank full of dimes on the coffee table. The bank was made of thick glass and had raised lettering that spelled "ESSO." I began experimenting and found that if I inserted a table knife in the slot I could carefully pull the knife out of the bank with the dimes on it. I felt bad about stealing four to five dimes a day, but that was enough to purchase bubble gum, tonic and a comic book from a little store at the corner. The young guy who ran the store had chased me away when I was checking the place out earlier. He said he didn't want me hanging around the store if I didn't have any money. He was a city boy and a smart-ass. Now that I had money, I'd hesitate buying something until he was about to open his big mouth and then I'd produce the money.

He asked, "Where are you getting the dough, Kid?"

I said, "None of your bees wax." I thought that my comment was really tough and I put Mr. Smart Ass in his place.

On the way back to Spring Gap on a Sunday, Buss told me that his job exemption from the draft would run out in a couple of weeks and then he would be drafted, probably before the year was out. Betty said she would continue staying at the trailer and working at the defense plant.

One evening, after a hard day of harvesting, Dad, Jesse and I were sitting on the tailgate of the pickup taking a break. Dad began to talk, an unusual experience for he seldom talked about anything except the work at hand. He said, "You boys should do everything you can to stay in school and finish high school. You don't want to hang around here and take up farming. If you do, you'll end up following a mule's ass behind a plow trying to scratch out a living on this damn rocky mountain."

He also told us: "Sharecroppers on a place like this are only able to make enough to care for their family, no matter what the shares. I will never make enough to own my own place. Hell, I don't even have a checking account."

I wondered later about Dad's statements. I didn't say anything to him at the time and later I asked Jesse if he knew why Dad said what he did. I figured it wasn't about me for I loved school and had no intention of quitting. Jesse said, "It's because I mentioned to him that I wanted to quit school."

I said, "You don't want to do that 'cuz you will be drafted immediately."

Jesse didn't comment.

Little Jersey was about ready to have her calf. She was huge and Dad thought that she might have twins. He took her out of the lot and put her in one side of the mule shed, which he had partitioned off from the hay storage part. Dad was afraid that Little Jersey would slip on the ice and snow or be butted by one of the other cows and be injured and lose her calf. She would remain in her new stall until after her calf was born.

The next morning when Jesse opened the door to give Little Jersey some water and feed, he found her lying down and having difficulty breathing. Jesse called for Dad to come and Dad took one look and knew what was likely wrong. She had pushed a board loose and had eaten almost a bag of oats and he figured she was foundered. This meant that gas from the fermenting oats had caused such great pressure that her two-stomach digestive system was not working. Dad called this condition "losing her cud." He explained that cows don't chew their food when they graze; they wad the grass into a ball and swallow the "cud" into the first stomach. Later, the cow lies down and belches up the cud from the first stomach, chews it, and swallows it again into the second stomach for digesting. Dad balled up a sock to make an artificial cud, lubricated the sock with lard, and tried to get Little Jersey to swallow it in the hope that her digestive system would start working, but she wouldn't swallow it.

Dad got in his truck and went for the vet. When they returned, Little Jersey's tongue was hanging out and she was gasping. The vet said that the action he had to take to release the gas from Little Jersey's stomach might kill her and the calf could also die. The operation had to be done immediately. He was going to use a knife to rupture the stomach and release the gas, and then maybe he could get her digestive system working.

Little Jersey didn't live through the ordeal. When the vet opened her up he found that she was carrying twin calves and he was only able to save one. Johnnie Cake, as we named the survivor, was healthy and loved to eat. Jesse and I hand-fed her with a bottle. Jesse taught her to drink milk from a bucket by allowing her to suck his finger and then lowering his hand into a bucket of milk and removing his finger from the calf's mouth so she would drink from the bucket.

The war news was encouraging. Our forces were having some victories, our bombers and fighters were able to bomb some German cities and Japanese islands. The bombing of London was less frequent. There was a lot of talk that the only way to win the war in Europe was to invade the mainland. So many men in our area were being drafted that it was impossible to keep up with the names. At first, men didn't want to be drafted, but more and more when someone's buddy would get drafted the one that was going to be left behind would volunteer. Dad wasn't able to get any help. All able-bodied men could easily get a job at the Celanese plant or Kelly Springfield Tire in Cumberland. No one wanted to work as a farm hand. Women, too, could get work in the defense plants. All three of my sisters, Lena, Betty and Georgia were now working in defense plants near Baltimore.

Mr. Miller at the Consolidated Orchard Company told Dad that he doubted if he could harvest the apples because he couldn't get a crew together. He estimated that he would have 100,000 bushels of apples and without more workers he might only be able to harvest half of the crop.

Beginning the eighth grade was fun. We had three or four substitutes for the regular teachers who were being drafted. Mr. Reiter, our principal, was teaching now and I had him for geometry. Just as I was catching on to algebra, now I had to take geometry. Lucky for me, I was able to understand it.

I got off on the wrong foot with Mr. Reiter. One day when he was writing on the board and had his back turned I wriggled my ears to amuse some of my friends. They would snicker and giggle. Mr. Reiter turned around and faced me and instead of yelling at me, looked straight at me and wriggled his ears. He said, "There's only room in this class for one person that has the talent to wriggle his ears. Mr. Shipe, and you can either stop wriggling yours or leave this class permanently. What's your decision?"

I said, "I'll stop, sir."

After class I was asking around how Mr. Reiter knew that I was wriggling my ears. I learned from a friend that he could pick up the reflection of the class in his glasses when he was at the blackboard.

Mr. Reiter's wife had the reputation of being the toughest English teacher on God's earth. She was the high school's only English teacher, and taught English grammar all year long to every class from seventh to twelfth grade. There was no way to get around Mrs. Reiter because four years of English were required to graduate. I struggled and struggled and she kept pouring the work on. Mr. and Mrs. Reiter were too old to be drafted; they were there to stay.

One of my classmates at school, Betty Rempher, was beautiful and had long black hair. We enjoyed doing crazy things and laughing together at most anything. She was a tomboy who loved to wrestle and she could take down almost everyone in our class. I didn't mind being wrestled to the ground by her.

One day, a substitute teacher who was a retired Methodist minister and who had been gassed during World War I caught five or six of us making fun of him as he tried to write something on the blackboard and couldn't remember how to spell the words. Our punishment was to stand in front of the class while he made us eat soap. When Betty's turn came, she couldn't stop laughing. She was spitting the soap out and the teacher kept cutting off a chunk of Lifebuoy and trying to make her eat it. She laughed until she wet her pants, which caused a puddle on the floor. Then she became angry and ran out of the room. It wasn't long before I got my turn and we both became members of the Lifebuoy soap gang.

One afternoon when the final bell rang I was walking down the hall and saw Betty standing at her locker. A great scheme came into my head. I thought that if I could push Betty into her locker and slam the door she would then have to scream and yell and beg me to come to her rescue. I gave her a big shove but she grabbed the sides of the locker and stiffened her arms. My scheme had failed! I turned her loose and she began chasing after me and throwing books and stuff at me so I ran into our homeroom. Dewey Deffinbaugh, the janitor, was starting to clean up and had moved the desks to one side of the room. Betty was hot on my tail so I jumped on the armrest of a desk, planning to jump from desk to desk and find safety in the back of the room. The first desk that I jumped onto tipped over and threw me onto the floor. I heard a "snap" and when I started to get up, I became acutely aware that some bones in my right arm had broken. Betty saw my arm and ran screaming from the room. Mr. Skidmore, a teacher, came into the room and when he saw my broken arm, asked Dewey to get a first-aid kit and then applied a splint. I had a compound fracture about two inches above my wrist. Teachers arranged for me to ride to Memorial Hospital in Cumberland with Mr. and Mrs. Reiter and he scolded me for my behavior all the way to the hospital.

The doctors in the emergency room wouldn't set my arm without my parent's permission. While I was lying on a flat table a man came in and asked me how I broke my arm. He wasn't concerned about whether I was in pain, which I was. He listened while I told him a fabricated story, a big lie.

I laid in the emergency room until Mom and Dad came, nearly four hours after I had fallen. Mom told me that Mrs. Gilbert Miller had come to our house and told her that the teachers from school had taken me to Memorial Hospital and for her not to worry, for I would be in good hands.

Mom gave permission for the doctors to set my arm and when I awoke, I was sick from the smell of ether and I wanted to gag. I had a big white cast on my right arm, from my knuckles to my armpit. They decided to keep me in the hospital overnight.

The next day, after Mom and Dad got me home, I went into the living room with them to relax. Dad brought a copy of *The Cumberland Evening Times* and divided the paper with Mom. She had her favorite parts of the paper to read first: who had died, who was visiting the area, and who had been admitted to the hospital or released. After a bit, Mom gave a gasp and said, "Did you tell this story to the newspaper?

I answered, "Tell what?"

Mom read:

"DAYDREAMER BREAKS ARM. Kenneth Shipe of Spring Gap was admitted to Memorial Hospital emergency room yesterday. He said that he was sitting at his desk at Oldtown School waiting for his bus to take him home. The warm afternoon sun shining in the classroom window made him sleepy. He dozed off, fell out of his chair and received a compound fracture of his right arm. He was released today."

I looked at Mom and Dad and said, "I have no regrets for telling that story." I explained that I didn't know that I was talking to a newspaper reporter. Further, I didn't believe a reporter should be in the emergency room interviewing patients. And, above all, I had made up my mind not to involve my school friend, Betty.

Mom said, "You lied, didn't you?"

"Yes," I replied. "And I'll do it again, 'cuz its not a stranger's business how I broke my arm."

Dad said, "Pearl, the boy has a good point. Newspaper reporters have no place in the hospital talking to kids."

I believe that was the most non-farm conversation that I had heard Dad say in all my born days. Mom was taken aback because Dad had chimed in with his opinion on a touchy matter like lying versus creating gossip.

The next day at school everyone was giving me a hard time. They knew that Betty ran me down and my arm broke when I fell from the chair, and they had heard about or read the newspaper article. Betty said she was sorry for running out of the room and not helping me. She said the sight of my arm broken was more than she could handle.

The teachers told me I would have to learn to write with my left hand or lose eight weeks of work, which could greatly impact my grades. All the teachers scolded me for my outrageous scheme to trap Betty in her locker. I began to realize how old-fashioned my teachers were becoming.

My brother, Pvt. Jesse E. Shipe—1944

Jesse quit school and the Draft Board called him for his physical. He was classified 1-A and received orders to report to the Army Induction Center in Baltimore.

Dad parked the truck in the Queen City Railroad Station lot and Mom and I went to the train with Jesse. A number of trains filled with soldiers were entering and leaving the station. All the men from one train were being lined up on the platform. Their leaders marched them to a field next to the station where they did some brisk exercises. Someone told Mom that the men had been on the train for more than a week, because they had come from Ft. Ord, California, on their way to Fort Meade, Maryland.

The moment I dreaded came. Jesse's train was about to leave and when he hugged Mom, she began crying and so did I. Poor Jesse, he tried as hard as he could, but all three of us were crying and we couldn't speak. Mom and I waved goodbye as the train pulled out.

Riding home, I sat up front with Mom and Dad and none of us spoke. The war had reached our family's flesh and blood.

My brother Bill and his wife came by our house a week after Jesse had left. Bill informed us that he was classified 1-A and would report to duty right away. Mom was having a very difficult time seeing her boys going off to war.

My brother, Pvt. William Shipe—1944

We bought a little flag with two blue stars and hung it in our window. Almost every home in the area had service flags in their windows.

Our Christmas was not joyous like Christmases past. Jesse, Bill, Robert Lee, Buss, and Mom's brothers, John and Jim, were all in the service and none would be able to come home. I asked for and got some nice clothes for Christmas. My sisters were teaching me how to mix and match pants and shirts; they knew a lot about which colors matched and which didn't.

10

Farm gives way to orchard

I didn't know anything about the big changes that were occurring at our place. However, I had noticed that a D-8 Caterpillar bulldozer owned by the Consolidated Orchard Company was often parked on the Millholland property. I also noticed a ditch was being dug between the two properties along the top of the mountain and in front of our house. Dad said that the ditch would soon have a water pipe laid with connections to our house and we would have running water, just like the other homes on the Consolidated Orchard Company property. He didn't volunteer any additional information; it did raise a question in my mind of why the Orchard Company would be running water across the Millholland property.

We installed some new fences around the wooded area on the east side of the mountain. We knew that when mules were first put into a new pasture the animals would test the fences. Dad walked the new fence line and gave the okay to put the mules into the new pasture. We were awakened early the next morning by a man who lived on the Twiggtown Road who had come to tell us that three mules were standing in the road near Merle Reckley's home. The man said that one of the mules had an injured front leg. We quickly verified that our mules weren't in their pasture and got in the pickup and headed down the mountain. When we arrived at Merle Reckley's we saw our three mules, with Beck hobbling along on three legs. Her left front hoof was wobbling around like she had broken her ankle. Dad reached Beck, lifted her leg, and saw that she had a life-ending injury.

Dad had Wilbur Silber use the D-8 bulldozer to push out a trench for a grave for Beck, for we had to put her down. I was appointed to pull the trigger. After we returned from Beck's grave and I sat the rifle in the corner of the kitchen, I slouched in a chair at the kitchen table. Dad said to Mom, "We're going backward because now, with two mules, we only meet the minimum requirements to be sharecroppers—a man with two mules and a plow."

Dad began a project to clear some new ground, a ten-acre section that separated the Consolidated Orchard property from the Millholland property located up the mountain, north beyond our house. He didn't use the Model "A" tractor rig to pull stumps; Wilbur Silber used the D-8 bulldozer. Dad used Jack and Belle to pull the uprooted stumps to the center of the new ground area, where he was burning them.

One afternoon after I got off the school bus, I noted that a huge hole had been gouged out of the ground by a bulldozer between the cottage in the field and the mule and cow shed. I went running into the house and confronted Mom about the dig.

Mom, Pearl Amanda Shipe, knew God and His ways.

She informed me that Mr. Millholland was working on a deal to sell his property to the Consolidated Orchard Company and this place would eventually be planted totally in orchard. Mom said, "Now you must not try to explain this to anyone, for all of the details haven't been worked out, so it's best to keep quiet about it."

Mom added: "Dad has been guaranteed a home place as long as he wants to live here and remains employed at the Consolidated Orchard. He will also be able to keep all of the animals as long as their fences and shelters don't interfere with the orchard."

I asked, "Does this mean that Dad will have a permanent day job?"

Mom answered, "Yes, and at present, the plan calls for the cottage in the field to be remodeled and relocated where the foundation has been dug. Then the old middle house and some of the sheds will also be torn down to make room for apple trees. After the cottage has been placed on the new foundation and remodeled, we will move into it, then this house will be remodeled, and afterward we will move back here. The plan calls for adding an upstairs on both houses and creating additional bedrooms.

"Now that's enough for now, okay?"

I answered, "Yes, but what really caused all the change?"

Mom said, "I think it had to do with the Government Farm Program and the loan that Mr. Millholland had. He had to make a profit and I don't believe the farm operation made an adequate profit. Now in wartime and without Jesse or any other help, Dad could not make this place profitable."

I responded, "I don't believe any sharecropper could ever make a profit on mountaintop land like this place. Dad has carried a heavy burden and nearly killed himself in trying to satisfy the landowner and the government, in a sharecropping scheme that had little chance of making it."

I walked out to where the foundation for the cottage had been dug. I began to imagine what this place was going to look like and the impact on my life. I went to a special place in the mule shed hayloft, a place where I could think, a place where the barn cats and kittens curled up beside me and purred while I thought things out about school, chores, girls and the future. I headed there because I needed to think about all of this, for I was sure Dad and Mom would not discuss this issue and its impact on me; they hated answering specific questions about the future and things that they couldn't control.

While lying in the hay I decided to build three lists in my mind on what the changes could mean: a "good list", a "bad list" and a "don't know list."

I started with the good list:

1. It would provide a permanent day job with a steady income, and a guaranteed place to live for Dad & Mom.

2. Mom would have a remodeled, almost new house, and there would be room for each of us to have our own bed. We would have electricity and water. We would still have an outhouse and Mom would still continue heating water in outside pots for washing clothes.

3. We would be able to have animals for milk and meat and our own garden spot.

4. I might be able to get some work for pay at the orchard.

5. We would have neighbors, possibly a pretty girl living next door. That would really be nice.

6. I could forget about being a sharecropper at this place.

The bad list:

1. There would be a big change: living from paycheck to paycheck, versus crop-to-crop and season-to-season. It would be a whole new way of life for us, like starting over. Our roots would be pulled from the soil, and our family heritage would wilt like a plant when its roots are exposed after a heavy rain.

The don't know list:

1. If a pretty girl moves next door, how am I supposed to involve her in some of my plans?

2. How can I obtain enough money on my own to get to college?

About this time I heard an airplane overhead. I ran outside and saw a yellow biplane coming in very low over the hay field. Was it going to crash? Oh my God, it landed!

I ran as hard I could to the field waving my arms frantically as the plane slowed and stopped. It was a yellow Stearman biplane, an early Army Air Force trainer and a great stunt plane. The pilot shut down his engine, climbed out of the cockpit, and said, "Hey, how you doing. I'm Robert Stewart. Is the big orchard to the north the Consolidated Orchard Company?"

I replied, "I'm Kenneth Shipe and yes, that's the Consolidated Orchard Company. You sure have a nice airplane."

Dad, Robert and me beside the plane

Robert said, "I do crop dusting and I hope to convince them that I can dust their fruit trees cheaper than their spraying methods. Have you ever been up in an airplane?"

I answered, "No, but it is my dream. I have all the Civil Air Defense Home Warden Aircraft Spotter Cards and I think I can identify every airplane that has flown over our place."

Dad was walking toward us and after a discussion he arranged for Robert to spend the night and make contact with Mr. Gilbert Miller, the Consolidated Orchard Company owner's son and general manager, the next morning. Robert offered Dad a ride and he immediately refused but told him that I was crazy about airplanes and might want a ride.

Robert said, "Hey Ken, we have a couple hours of sunshine and I have to fly to Mexico Farms Field to gas up, so jump in and we'll go for a spin."

I was speechless, and scared. The plane had two cockpits behind its double wings and I stuffed my cap in my hip pocket and climbed in the front cockpit. Robert strapped me in and explained about the rudder pedals and the stick. He said, "This plane can be controlled from either cockpit, but I'll do all of flying."

I knew a little about the control surfaces of aircraft and the flight controls because I had read many articles about aircraft in *Popular Mechanics* magazines.

We taxied uphill to the end of the hayfield and turned around heading downhill. Robert set the engine at full throttle. The wind from the propeller blew my hair and the roar of the engine made the plane vibrate so much that I had trouble focusing my eyes. Robert released the brakes and we bounced down the pasture. The grass became a blur and then the electric poles were zipping by too fast to count and the plane leaped into the air. Robert circled over our place a couple of times. I could see Mom and Dad waving at us. Robert rocked the wings of the plane from side to side to signal that he recognized their waves. We flew north along the mountain. The rows of apple trees seemed so uniform and perfectly spaced in a pattern that looked like a hand-sewn quilt. We turned northwest and headed toward Mexico Farms Field, about five miles from our house as the crow flies.

We circled the smooth grass field and landed as gently as a maple leaf falling from a tree. We rolled to a stop near the gas pumps and climbed out of the cockpits. I was so excited I could barely breath; this was the greatest moment in all my born days! I could tell that the guys around the airport were looking at me and wishing they could fly in the beautiful big Stearman, which was an early Army Air Force trainer that possessed great stunt-flying capabilities.

Robert fueled the airplane, checked the oil and did a complete preflight inspection. As he checked each item he explained to me its function and why it was critical for a good pilot to personally use his eyes to look and his hands to touch various features before each and every flight.

Robert asked, "Do you know the basics of flight controls like pitch, yaw and roll attitudes?"

I answered, "Yes sir."

Then he said, "Okay, explain the controls you would move to go up, then down, then left and then right."

So I explained how the stick controlled the tail elevator for up and down. The ailerons and foot pedals controlled the rudder for yaw and the stick and pedals worked together to roll the airplane and make turns.

Robert reviewed a set of rules for me to follow when we were in the air: he would wriggle the stick for me to take over the controls and he would pound on the side of the plane when he wanted to take control back.

But the first thing he wanted to do was fly to 10,000 feet and do some rolls, loops, spins and stalls. Robert saw that I was very nervous and shaking a little and he asked, "Y'all right?"

I answered, "I'm shaking because I have to take a leak."

He said, "Go around the corner of the hanger."

I had a few moments to gather my thoughts. My stomach was rolling. I was so excited I puked right there beside the hanger. Now I was feeling much better. I could fly now.

Up into the sky we went. I survived the aerobatics because Robert flew the plane so well that even when upside down I remained fast to the bottom of the seat. I didn't even feel a little bit sick. Then the biggest moment of my young life: Robert shook the stick and I took control of the airplane. It was difficult keeping the plane straight and level and I felt Robert's corrections on the stick and rudder pedals, but soon I had a sense of how to look out at the horizon and keep the wings and nose level. I began using the artificial horizon instrument's ball indicator to stay level and the altimeter to maintain altitude. I banked the plane very slowly in a wide circle to the left and then leveled out and turned right, keeping the nose from dropping or lifting in the turns. This was so great! I knew I was flying on my own for Robert wasn't nudging the controls as he had earlier.

After three times doing the basic maneuvers, Robert slapped the side of the plane and I could feel him take control. The sun was setting. What a great view of the beautiful scene below—the Potomac River Valley between Short Gap, West Virginia, and Spring Gap, Maryland. We landed back at our hayfield and rolled to a stop. I sat there in the cockpit for a moment trying to take in all that had happened to me in the last two hours, the smell of the engine exhaust, the sounds of the engine cooling. This was all like a dream.

Dad said, "How did you like that?"

I responded: "I'll never look at a flying hawk or buzzard the same as I used to. I would love to be flying with them."

I knew then what I wanted to do—FLY AIRPLANES! Either be a crop duster or a fighter pilot and fly a U.S. Army Air Force P-38 Lightning!

The next morning, Dad drove Robert to meet Mr. Miller and they were back in about an hour. Robert said that Mr. Miller wasn't interested in aircraft dusting of his orchard at this time.

I thanked Robert as best as I could for the plane ride and the opportunity to fly his aircraft. He said he believed I would make a good pilot someday and that it was possible for me to get a book and learn to fly by age fourteen.

We watched the biplane take off. As it climbed Robert saluted us from the cockpit then turned toward Cumberland and was soon out of sight.

No longer would our hayfield be a hayfield to me. I imagined I would be taking daily flights to wonderful places right from Shipe Farm Airfield.

I was writing to Jesse almost every week. He had finished his basic training at South Camp Hood, Texas, and was coming home for a furlough. We couldn't wait to see him. When he arrived home he looked great in his uniform and had a great suntan. He was rock-solid, about 210 pounds. He brought me a leather wallet made of cowhide that had red and white hair, like it had come from a Hereford steer.

Jesse had his orders to report to North Camp Hood, Texas, and believed that he was going into a mechanized infantry unit of armored tank destroyers. He also thought that he would be going overseas almost as soon he returned and finished his training as a tank destroyer crewman.

It was tough for Mom when Jesse prepared to leave, much tougher than the first time he left. We knew that the Nazi and Japanese forces would not surrender until they were defeated on their own soil and that meant major invasions of foreign lands that would involve my brothers, Jesse and Bill.

The remodeling of the cottage was complete and we moved in. I slept upstairs, in my own bed, alone. The house smelled of new paint and the doors and windows all shut and opened easily and stayed latched. We had electricity. Mom and Dad kept reminding me to turn off the lights. The light bill was going to be their first monthly bill and they were greatly concerned about it. I loved the brightness of electric lights, and being able to read in good light changed things for me. I began to add extension cords from the ceiling receptacle to a bedside lamp. We had an electric radio, which made a huge change in our home life. The radio was on almost all the time, because we didn't have to worry about the batteries dying.

My buddy, Kenneth Cage, hadn't been to school for a couple of days. When he did return, he informed everyone that his home had burned down and his family members would have to be placed in various homes until a place to live was found. He would more than likely have to move to Cumberland and change schools. I told Mom and she didn't hesitate a minute; she said that Kenneth could come to live with us as long as he needed. So Kenneth brought the few clothes he had and we were roommates.

Since Kenneth had spent many weekends at my house we already knew what was expected of us and had only a few details to work out for dividing up the chores. I knew that this arrangement was going to be great because my chore load would be less.

Mom and Dad considered Kenneth a family member. If Mom bought either of us a new outfit she bought both of us the same thing. We often dressed alike, same color pants and shirts, even penny loafers alike. Kenneth placed a penny in the keeper strap on his loafers but I liked the shine of a dime, so we were different in that one respect. When we got dressed up in our new clothes, we sensed that the mountain wasn't big enough to hold us.

We both worked hard to earn enough money and remain in good standing with Dad and Mom so that we could go to town each Saturday night to see a show at the Strand Theater. We became hooked on the serials and we worked our tails off so that we wouldn't miss the continuation of a serial from Saturday to

Saturday. Tom Mix, The Lone Ranger, Gene Autry and the music of the Sons of the Pioneers were among our favorite movie characters.

Kenneth and I began to identify with the cowboy serial characters. One day we were looking around in Rosenbaum's department store and spotted a set of cowboy belts with cap pistols that were so realistic we thought they were real, and we had to have them. They cost about half the price of a new bicycle. We inquired about lay-a-way but the clerk wouldn't put them on lay-away without an adult signing, so we looked for Mom. She was already at the Cooperative Feed Store parking lot and Dad was ready to go home. We convinced Mom to put the guns on lay-away until we could earn the money to pay for them. Mom couldn't believe two boys as old as us had to have toy gun belts, but we "stuck to our guns" on this one. We earned the money and soon had our cap pistols and plenty of caps and we played cowboys and Indians around the farm, being mindful not to let certain teasing adults know that boys our age were playing with toy guns.

The remodeling job complete, my family moved back into our original house. The outside was covered with white asbestos shingles and we had new windows, new doors, a new porch on the north side and a new entry door at the west. The floors had been sanded and varnished and we had new linoleum in the kitchen. A stairway ran down from the kitchen to the basement and we had a stairway upstairs from the kitchen. Mom had a sink in her kitchen with cold running water. Our home now had electricity—but we still had the outside privvy, washed our hands and faces in basins on the porch, and bathed in #10 washtubs by the kitchen stove.

Kenneth and I had a very large unfinished upstairs area. We found some used linoleum covering from the old kitchen floor to put down and we stacked apple boxes to store our underwear and socks. We strung a rope clothesline across two rafters to hang our pants and shirts. The windows in the ends of the house provided views across the mountains and excellent ventilation.

Dad continued to clear the ten acres of new ground between the orchard and the Millholland place. He offered Kenneth and me jobs dragging brush into a pile for burning. The fallen trees were loaded with vines and since it was late winter we didn't have to concern ourselves with leaves and the like, we just kept the fire very hot and everything we threw into it was quickly consumed.

On a Sunday evening, after Kenneth and I had been working all day Saturday burning brush, we broke out with a bumpy rash on our arms and face. We both were scratching and when we awoke Monday morning our eyes were swollen shut. Mom took one look at us and said, "You both have poison oak and probably one of the worst cases I have ever seen." The rash was on our scalp, hands, arms, belly, legs, face and worst of all, on our private parts. That's where it itched the most. Mom gave us some calamine lotion to help with the itching but it didn't help much. We dampened our skin and applied baking soda and that didn't help. We had scratched ourselves until a watery substance was oozing from the burst blisters. The worst itching was on our scrotum; we couldn't stop scratching there. It hurt awful to scratch—and at the same time it felt good when we did.

We decided to make a mixture of the things we had been using individually and hope for a cure. Our reasoning was that if one ingredient helped a little then a mixture would work two or three times better and who knows, maybe, we'd be cured. We added to the calamine lotion some wintergreen oil, baking soda, water, lye soap and turpentine. The mixture bubbled at first, and when it quit bubbling, turned brown. We both stripped naked and sat on the edge of the bed. Using cotton balls, we dabbed the mixture over the parts of our bodies that we could reach, and then helped each other with our backsides.

At first we felt better, at least we weren't as itchy. But soon our scrotum sacks began to burn and then we couldn't stand it and we were dancing around our bedroom like Indians on the warpath. After a bit, Kenneth yelled toward the downstairs to Mom, "Hide your eyes Pearlzie, here we come!" (Pearlzie was an endearing name that Kenneth called Mom.) He hit the door at the bottom of the stairs and busted the door jam right off and the falling door hit the new refrigerator and damaged it. We both ran outside, naked, to the cistern water pump and began pumping water into the ladle and throwing the water on our bodies. It was freezing cold outside but we kept splashing water onto ourselves. We had to stop the water treatment because we were too cold. Mom threw some blankets onto the porch and they hid our nakedness, but the terrible burning continued.

We managed to get back upstairs and under the covers to warm up. The burning lasted for hours. We were beet red, sick to our stomachs, and suffering terribly with chills. Mom was afraid that we needed to go to the hospital but we elected to tough it out.

The next morning we were some better. The blisters had broken and our skin was dry. The third day we were much better and our skin started to peel. We peeled for days.

11

Demise of the three-hole privvy

The troop trains were rumbling day and night on both sides of the Potomac River, the Western Maryland Railroad on the Maryland side and the Baltimore and Ohio Railroad on the West Virginia side. It seemed that every train either had troops or war equipment on it. Flat cars carried tanks, cannons, trucks and other military equipment. The war was heating up. Items in the stores were becoming scarce and rationing of gasoline, food and clothing was impacting all of us, but people around Spring Gap were not complaining because everyone knew that an all-out effort was under way to defeat our enemies. The major impact on my family was rationing of shoes and sugar. Dad used his shoe last and replaced soles and heals; the repair pieces were scarce but weren't rationed. Mom used less sugar for canning fruits and our apple butter wasn't as sweet as usual, but she knew how to increase the proportion of sweeter apples to keep it tasting good.

The Consolidated Orchard Company hired Kenneth and me as Saturday workers during school. We received 35 cents an hour and were very happy to have these jobs. In the winter we dragged brush from where the apple trees had been trimmed to a central spot for burning. Usually it was a wide spot in the road or a place where a dead tree had been removed and there was enough space for a fire. We had to be careful not to heat up the air too much because, according to Dad, the trees could come out of their dormancy and sap could start flowing. With sap up, the bark could split during a freeze. We were in the boys' work gang, made up of guys from the Spring Gap area. The trimming gang was made up of regular orchard workers who did the trimming of the trees, which required skill. A good trimmer did the obvious removal of dead and broken branches but after that he had to use judgment and experience to determine which limbs or branches to prune so that the new crop of apples would have the proper amount of sunlight and room to mature. The foreman, Turk Twigg, said, "Its like the difference between giving a tree a crew cut versus an adult trim cut." Dad was an excellent trimmer; he had good judgment in allowing for growth without pruning too many small branches with buds.

Columbus Delauder, the boss of the boys' gang, knew all of us well because most of us were members of his Sunday school class at Mt. Tabor Methodist Church. Columbus seldom missed a chance to do a little preaching to us, especially during breaks. We would pull up some apple boxes and sit in a circle during break and pass the common water jug and drink from it. None of us used two hands; we'd flip the jug on the outside of one arm and cradle the jug to our mouth and take a big swig. This was always followed by a big "Ahh!" Then we'd wipe our mouth on our sleeve.

Johnnie Cake, the calf that the veterinarian delivered when Little Jersey died in calf birth, was now about 300 pounds and even at her size she wanted to follow me everywhere. She loved to lick my skin to get the salt; her tongue was so rough I could barely stand it.

Me and Johnnie Cake, our beef calf.

Dad continued to warn me that I shouldn't make a pet out of Johnnie Cake. I began to realize how hard it would be to have an animal that was special and yet have to kill it for food. We all had trouble with this, even the killing of hogs and chickens for the dinner table, for we nurtured and cared for them, carrying food and water to them at least once and sometime twice a day. The animals knew us and would respond to us, showing excitement when we approached. Often they would forgo eating and come to us to be petted and they enjoyed hearing our voices. I figured this behavior showed that the animals saw us as a god, for they were dependent upon us for their daily bread and needs.

Kenneth and I began experimenting with smoking, chewing tobacco, and rubbing snuff. One day Dad sent us to the house to get a jug of drinking water and a can of snuff. We figured this would be a good time to try Scotch snuff. Many times we had seen Dad dip some from the can with his finger and place it between his lower lip and gum. We both took a big dip and rubbed it off onto our lip. We used our tongue to wallow it around, and soon we began spitting. We talked about how rotten it tasted and our tongue and inside of our mouth began to sting. We figured the best thing to do was take a big drink of water to flush the snuff out. But instead of spitting out the mess Kenneth swallowed. He began to gag and sputter and I thought he would throw up. He was white as a sheet. I flushed my mouth and spit on the ground, but enough snuff remained in my mouth to make me good and sick.

When we got to where Dad was working, he noted that we both looked pale. He said, "How did you like the snuff?"

Kenneth replied, "The darn stuff has made us sick and you won't have to worry about us dipping your snuff anymore."

Kenneth and I saved our money and bought a machine for rolling our own cigarettes. Erma at the Millstone store wouldn't sell cigarettes to us but we could purchase a can of tobacco and rolling papers. The machine had a place to mount a single sheet of cigarette paper into which we shook Prince Albert cut tobacco from a can, we then pulled a lever and out came a nice-looking cigarette. We made a batch of cigarettes and filled the empty tobacco cans with our smokes.

Right away, we lit up a cigarette and smoked. Kenneth had done some inhaling earlier and when he tried it again the smoke made him cough and sputter, but he put on a good front. He acted real hot about how good he could smoke. I faked inhaling for a long time.

We only smoked when we were out of sight of Mom. We knew that she would be terribly hurt that we were doing things to damage our bodies while she was doing everything in her power to keep us healthy. We stored the cigarette machine, tobacco and cans of cigarettes in a knothole in a peach tree near the house.

One day when we and our buddies were up on the mountain, we rolled a batch of cigarettes. As we were walking down the mountain all of us were smoking and inhaling except me. The others began to call me chicken so I took a big drag and inhaled. It was like swallowing fire. In all my born days I could never figure out why something that tasted so awful became something I couldn't stop doing.

One job that seemed to never end was hoeing corn in the field that ran south from the house all the way to the power lines. Each row of corn was about one mile long and the field was 35 rows wide. When the heat was getting to us and we were near the peach tree we got our smokes and headed for the outhouse, which was about 50 yards down the hill from the main house. It was an old building, made of rough-sawed slab boards. Because they were unfinished the boards had large cracks between them. The toilet had three holes. Kenneth sat on one of the adult holes and I sat on the other. We had our clothes on, for we were just using the place for a smoke break. To our surprise Mom yelled from the back porch, "What are you boys doing down there?" We threw the cigarettes into the toilet holes and fanned the smoke as hard as we could to get rid of it, and soon there was plenty of smoke boiling through the cracks and up through the roof vent.

We opened the door and smoke bellowed out and I yelled, "We were just taking a toilet break." We grabbed our hoes and chopped weeds as fast as we could, to get as much distance from the house as we could. Mom didn't come after us so we figured she didn't suspect that we were smoking, and we continued chopping weeds and back filling dirt around each stalk of corn. Then we heard a loud snapping and crackling noise coming from the direction of the outhouse and when we turned, we couldn't believe our eyes—the outhouse was on fire! Flames were shooting at least 50 feet in the air and the structure burned to the ground in just a few minutes.

Mom came running down the hill and yelled at us, "Now see what you've done. I knew you were allowing the devil his way with you. Wait 'til Dad sees this."

Mom went into the house, and we walked near where the fire was smoldering. A catalogue was on the ground, its pages being lifted by the breeze and burning individually as they turned. Kenneth said, "Boy, we've done it. We've burnt down the shithouse and John Russell will kill both of us." (John Russell was the name Kenneth called Dad.)

Mom told Dad and he was really angry. He said, "I want you boys to start before supper and dig a pit for a new toilet behind the smokehouse. It has to be six feet by six feet square and eight feet deep." And he added, "I don't give a damn if you have to dig day and night, because a new toilet will be here day after tomorrow by noon." We started digging with pick and two shovels, and when it got dark we lit lanterns and continued to dig without supper until we developed huge blisters on our hands and our backs were sore.

Herbie came out and added insult to injury when he said he had to poop and didn't have a place to go and it was all our fault since we burned down the toilet. We dug him a special hole in the dirt pile and after he finished we covered it up.

The next morning we circled the kitchen table for breakfast, but we knew from Mom's looks and actions that she wasn't going to fix us any food. We got a glass of milk and some homemade bread and spread butter and a little sugar on it. It tasted so good. Mom said, "Don't eat that whole loaf. That's all the bread we have and I don't bake for another day."

The pit wasn't finished by dark the second day. We continued into the night and finished around midnight. We were both exhausted. We never dreamed how difficult it would be to dig a pit eight feet deep. We had to use a ladder to get down into the hole to dig and at that depth only one could dig at a time. Our hands were raw in many places and some of the blisters had burst.

An Allegany County truck delivered a new toilet about noon. The toilet was prefabricated with siding that had very small pea rocks embedded in a composition board and it looked like it was made of tar and wood shavings pressed together. Dad helped the driver, Kenneth and me skid the toilet over some boards and level it over the pit. The driver said it was one of the best holes he had seen dug, since most people use a machine to dig their pits. Dad commented, "The boys did a damn good job. They are good workers." Kenneth and I almost fell over when Dad complemented us for our work.

The driver said, "Sorry I wasn't able to deliver the toilet two weeks earlier as promised, but the demand for free toilets is great in these parts."

Dad had a sheepish grin on his face when he said, "Boys, let's eat dinner and then bring Mom out to see the new privvy, Okay?" Kenneth and I gingerly washed our hands in the basin on the bench on the porch and we dried on the towel; our hands were raw.

Mom was proud of the new toilet. It had one seat, which was a store-bought one, nice and smooth. The old toilet seat had been rough as anything because the mice and rats had chewed at the edges. There was a toilet paper holder but we brought Spiegel, Montgomery Ward and Sears, Roebuck catalogues from the house as a supply of paper until Mom could buy some tissue from the store.

Dad said, "Get a halter and help me load Johnnie Cake into the pickup." His plan was to haul Johnnie Cake to the Taschenburger farm near Mexico Farms; they had a slaughterhouse in their barn. The Taschenburgers' had a deal where they would keep a certain amount of the meat to cover their butchering labor and purchase any remaining meat that we didn't want. Dad wanted to keep a hindquarter. Dad said to me, "I need your help to load Johnnie Cake, but you don't have to come with me to Taschenburger's."

I answered, "She has been mine to raise and I want to go with you."

Dad looked at me in a way that showed I had the critical decision to make and then he said, "Had Johnnie Cake been a pure bred you could have kept her for your school FFA and 4-H projects. She could have been shown at the fair. But since she isn't, and we haven't enough pasture for another milk cow, we'll have to butcher her for beef."

My heart was heavy when we loaded Johnnie Cake. She followed me onto the pickup just like she had always willingly followed me anywhere. The time driving up Highway 51 toward Cumberland went by fast. We turned into the lane at the farm and Dad drove up the barn ramp and stopped at the large double barn doors. Mr. Taschenburger wheeled up a portable ramp and I led Johnnie Cake off the pickup and inside. One of Mr. Taschenburgers' helpers, dressed in a white shop coat, approached me and without saying a word struck Johnnie Cake in the head with a large ball peen hammer. My calf fell straight down at my feet. I dropped the halter rope, took one last glance at the motionless Johnnie Cake, gave the bastard that hit Johnnie Cake a mean glare, and ran from the barn and jumped in the cab of the pickup.

We were a couple miles from the slaughterhouse when Dad spoke. "I had no idea he would kill her like that. I'm sorry. You shouldn't have come." I was crying dry tears; my stomach was so knotted I had trouble breathing. I didn't say anything back to Dad.

I knew that loving Johnnie Cake as much as I did involved a lesson that I had been warned about many times. I had known that the day would come for Johnnie Cake to be butchered, but I couldn't see the end. In all my born days I never imagined how life would teach this lesson. Johnnie Cake was family and it really hurt for a long time.

Dad had gone to the Post Office and got the mail for all the people living on the mountain. He had a letter from Jesse that Mom hurried to open. Jesse had written to let us know that his entire outfit and their equipment had been transferred from Texas and at the time of the writing he was in Fort Dix, New Jersey. He indicated that he was not supposed to talk too much about his whereabouts. Jesse asked for addresses of some of his school pals and girlfriends, so we figured his unit was on the East Coast and soon would be sent to Europe.

The Consolidated Orchard was hiring all the boys they could for Saturdays and for summer jobs. Kenneth and I were in spray crews. The orchard had a network of steel pipes throughout the orchard, with hose connections arranged in a grid so that the spray crews could attach 200-foot hoses. With this system all of the trees on the orchard could be sprayed. The spray chemicals were mixed and pumped from a building located on the north end of the orchard and the spray was delivered to the valves at a pressure of about 60 pounds per square inch.

A spray crew consisted of a gunner, a hose carrier and a back hose man. The gunner handled the gun that had six spray nozzles. The hose carrier stood behind the gunner and held the hose on his shoulder, allowing as much slack as he could between himself and the gunner and ensuring that the hose didn't drag on the ground. He remained at a distance behind the gunner so that the hose was free for the gunner to swing the gun and move in and out under and around the tree. The back hose man managed the remainder of the hose so that it never became tangled or twisted. The gunner was one of the regular orchard men while the other two jobs were assigned to the temporary help. The hose carrier was the worst job because this person had to anticipate the movements of the gunner and often the gunner would back up or swing the gun and hit the hose carrier.

During the spring a sulfur mixture was used on the trees prior to the leaves coming out, to reduce scale on the tree bark. This spray turned our skin and hair yellow. Having yellow hair was an indication that you had a paying job at the orchard; the girls at school didn't care for the yellow hair; they acted like we had some kind of disease.

We received good money from working on the orchard, and Kenneth and I were able to work a lot of hours during the summer months. We informed Mom and Dad that while we were working we would be responsible for purchasing all of our clothes for the new school year. Orchard work was the only paying job for boys around these parts but the hot days had us wondering if there were easier jobs somewhere else.

One day after work, four of us told the crew boss that we'd walk back to the work camp instead of riding the truck. We headed for the water reservoir at the spray shed. This reservoir stored water for mixing the chemicals. We stripped naked and were having a great time diving into the water from the roof of the spray shed. We swam and played in the water for about half an hour when Kenneth yelled, "Here comes a car!" We all jumped into the water and tried to lay low and the water level was about 12 inches below the edge of the wall. Bill Reckley said, "Oh my Lord, its Mrs. Miller and she's getting out of her car."

We treaded water while Mrs. Miller came to the edge of the reservoir. She lectured us about how dangerous it was for us to be swimming in a remote place like this with none of us trained as lifeguards. We thought she would never stop talking and leave. She knew we were naked because she was standing within a couple feet of our clothes. This was a serious situation, for Mrs. Miller was the wife of one of the owners of the orchard. We had to keep our mouths shut and hope she wouldn't tell her husband, Gib. Nothing was ever mentioned about the incident and we were happy we still had our jobs.

Kenneth and I were ready for school. Having money enough to buy clothes and some to save was good, but we were tired of working six days a week and school was a welcome change. Our school had many substitute teachers because most of the young and middle-aged men teachers had been drafted. Many of the women teachers had left to follow their husbands or to work in higher-paying defense plant jobs.

In February of 1945 we had one of the worst ice storms anyone had ever seen around our parts. We had about four inches of snow then it warmed, melting the snow a little, and then it turned cold and froze a hard crust on the snow. It began as rain with temperatures at freezing, temperatures again dropped below freezing and hovered around zero for weeks. We had ice that could be measured in inches thick.

Dad fashioned spiked heels for our shoes just so that we could get around. From old shoes, he removed rubber heels and drove nails outward through the heel and then attached that heel with nails onto the heels of our regular shoes.

The new shed for mules and cows was below the house on the east side of the mountain and it was treacherous carrying water down there with the ice covering everything.

We had a young heifer named Jill; she was the seventh female calf from Grannie. The cows had a small feedlot on the side. The lot fence was made from log slabs nailed to wooden posts. I let the cows out so that I could clean the stalls. The cows had been penned up for a few days, and when I opened the door Jill bolted from the shed, hit the ice went flat on her side, began skidding downhill toward the fence, and hit it hard. The boards were knocked from the posts and Jill slid down the side of the mountain until she was lodged against a stand of small trees. She was about 30 yards away from the cowshed. She was in a pickle; she couldn't come back up the mountain for it was too icy and couldn't go down without danger of another long slide to the next stand of trees.

I asked Dad, "What in the world are we going to do? Jill can't get back up to the barn and we can't get down there to feed her."

He said, "I feel like saying 'to hell with her,' but maybe you should slide some corn fodder down to her to eat. She'll have to lick the ice for water."

Jill was down the side of the mountain stuck in the trees for three days and joined the other cows after the ice melted.

An unusually shaped letter came in the mail. Mom knew it was about Jesse, but she had never seen a letter like it. It was about four inches square and had a window in the envelope to view the mailing and return addresses. I'm sure she thought it was a telegram from the War Department. She asked me to open it. It was a V-mail letter. The V-mail was a photograph of a letter from Jesse. The War Department processed all military mail from Europe to the U.S. using a microfiche film process. Jesse said he had landed on D-Day in the southern part of France and was somewhere in France and had seen enough combat, mud, stuck tanks and equipment to last him a lifetime. He wanted cookies and any kind of food that we could mail to him. He had been on K rations and C rations. His letter said that the French farmers were in bad shape. Most of their homes had damage and their crops were poor for June. In the towns the cobblestone streets were so narrow that often the tanks couldn't turn the corners and many times they took the corner of a building down and messed up the cobblestone streets as they turned. We were all relieved that he was okay. I wrote to him almost every week. He said he barely had time to write, but loved all the letters from home.

Mr. House, my 4-H and FFA (Future Farmers of America) teacher, passed out a piece of paper about a two-week summer camp to be held at Deep Creek Lake, Maryland. The price was 20 dollars. I showed the announcement to Mom, and to my surprise she was for it. She said, "I don't want you to work all during your school vacation like you have been doing. If you aren't careful you'll grow up to be like your father, who hasn't taken a vacation in his whole life."

Elated, I said, "I can't wait." I noted that the camp had a lot of competitive stuff like riflery, swimming, horseshoes and softball. Mr. House would see that transportation would be available when the time comes. The camp was a former CCC camp with cabins, mess hall and a lot of activity buildings and the lake had a great boat dock as well as swimming.

Mr. House also sent a note to my parents and me, urging us to begin thinking of a 4-H and FFA project for the coming year. Growing and showing small vegetables would not be enough to earn a good grade, he suggested, and since we had the pastures, growing a pure-bred beef or a pure bred hog would be an ideal project.

Mom thought it would be a good idea to grow and show a hog. I told Mom that a pure-bred animal could cost four or five times what an unregistered one would cost. But she said she wanted me to have a project animal.

After the Johnnie Cake incident, I wasn't sure if I wanted to get involved with another animal. I knew that showing animals required a lot of attention, and training them for the show ring required a lot of time. I didn't push the issue.

When Dad heard about the letter from Mr. House he was all for getting a pure-bred pig. "If you get a shoat it would be about two months old, and it would be a little over one year old when the fair starts next year."

I found myself in an unusual position—the first time I didn't have to push for something that cost a lot of money. I wanted the pig but I wasn't sure how to walk the fine line of not getting too close to an animal that eventually will end up butchered. I decided that I could do it, and began showing interest in the project by cutting out pictures of various breeds of hogs. Dad wanted to help with the decision and he and Mom enjoyed making suggestions on which would be the right choice from the pictures. After about a month we came up with the Hampshire breed, a black hog with a white band around its front quarters.

I checked with Mr. House and he said that the breed was a good choice, not only for its meat but also because the hogs had good proportional characteristics. The black with a white band showed well, especially, in head-to-head competition with single-color breeds.

I pondered why Mom and Dad were encouraging me to do 4-H and FFA projects at a time when our lives were moving away from farming to hourly work at the orchard. Perhaps showing hogs at the fair appealed to them, for they only knew the meat aspect of raising hogs and had never experienced the competitiveness of showing animals.

12

Lessons learned from farm animals

As I was getting off the bus I noticed a pickup parked near the mule shed and a stranger talking to Dad. After I changed into work clothes I headed over there. It was the vet talking to Dad.

Dad said, "Don't go in the barn just yet." I knew the 'just yet' was a clue that something very bad was wrong with one of our large animals. Dad's actions spoke volumes. His manner showed that he was deeply concerned, like when matters concerning life issues were heavy upon his heart.

Dad called me to his side and said, "Belle apparently caught her front foot under an exposed tree root on one of the sloping trails in the pasture. Her ankle wasn't strong enough to stop her as her body weight pushed against the root. The break is so bad she will have to be put down."

I ran into the barn and Belle looked around at me just as the vet lifted her leg. I could see that her ankle was wobbling around as if only the skin was holding her foot to her leg. It was obvious that Belle was in pain; her eyes were soulful and she had her ears turned back. The vet gave Belle a shot to ease her pain.

Dad asked the vet to make arrangements to have Belle's carcass delivered to a fertilizer plant.

None of the family could eat supper. We all found it difficult to talk about Belle's accident. Dad broke the silence and said, "Belle was the best mule I ever owned and she has been a faithful worker for our family for over fourteen years." He recalled how the white stripe of hair along Belle's back was caused from an electric shock when she rubbed against a bare wire in the ceiling of a mine. After that she refused to enter a mine and was useless for mine work. "I bought her for five dollars and it was the best five-dollar investment I ever made."

The fertilizer plant man came the next day. We heard the shot and watched the truck as it pulled out from the mule shed, turned left and drove out of sight.

I said to Dad, "You can only use a single-point plow now that we only have one mule."

Dad replied, "Jack, the ornery bastard, will be impossible to work now that he knows he is the only mule. He'll act like he deserves special treatment."

But during the months after Belle's death Jack became friendlier to any of us who went near where he was pastured. The cows hated him, because if they came near he would lay his ears back and bite them on the rump, and if they crossed behind him too close he would rear his hind legs and give them a kick. Jack's only friends were family members and a couple of barn cats. He would bray and bray if he saw any of us out and about, and if we sat on the porch of the house he wouldn't stop until someone went down to talk to him. Jack was a lonely mule.

Even though Jack and Dad were on better terms, an incident occurred one morning while Dad was harnessing Jack. Dad had put the collar on Jack, and was swinging the harness onto the mule's back. At that instant, Jack leaned against Dad and pinned Dad against the stall wall and was using his body weight to keep Dad there. Dad was yelling and cussing up a storm, kicking Jack's ribs with his knees and pounding on the mule's back with his fists. But Jack continued to apply just enough pressure to keep Dad pinned. I was watching all this from above in the haymow, where I was putting hay down into Jack's manger. I jumped into the stall in front of Jack and yelled, "Back up!" Jack stepped to the other side of the stall and he was prancing around like he had happy feet. Dad fretted and cussed until he ran out of words. I fastened the bellyband and tightened the hames strap around the collar and made sure Jack was properly harnessed. Then Dad said, "Take the damn harness off, I've changed my mind. I'm not going to work him today."

I sensed that Jack had awaited his opportunity to get Dad's full attention in such a way that he didn't hurt his good buddy and that there would never be anything either Jack or Dad could do to improve their relationship.

Kenneth and I were late getting our chores done and we began eating supper at about the time Mom and Dad were finishing theirs. I could tell by the way Mom and Dad were looking at each other that they had something up their sleeves and were bursting to tell us. Either they had found out something about my behavior or they knew a secret; they had a way of telegraphing news by their actions. And Dad seldom hung around the kitchen after supper. Then I heard "oink, oink" coming from behind the stove. Kenneth and I looked and there was my six-week old Hampshire pig—a beauty, black with a perfect white stripe around her shoulders. Dad had the information and forms for me to register the pig with the Hampshire Swine Breeders Association.

A while later the papers came in the mail and on the fancy certificate was the name *Gladheart Lady Olive's Best*. We all got a chuckle out of the long handle the Association gave her. Dad wanted to know what I was going to call her. I thought about that for a while. The heartbreak experience of naming Johnnie Cake was fresh in my mind and it had taught me a hard lesson about naming animals that would one day be butchered.

Mom sensed that I was reluctant to name her, so she suggested, "You should call her Lady."

"Okay," I said. "That's fine with me."

Against all that we had learned about raising animals, Lady became the family's pet. We kept Lady behind the kitchen stove for a couple of days, and then we moved her to her own pen and made a warm nest from straw. All visitors to our place were taken to see Lady and told that she would be shown at the county fair next year.

We hadn't heard from Jesse for months. Then a short V-mail note told us that he was okay and that he had been on the front lines, surrounded for 99 days straight at the Battle of the Bulge, in Belgium. He asked Mom to send some cookies and anything else homemade and suggested sending them packed in meat tins to withstand the rough treatment of mail handlers. He wrote that he had been involved in the capture of some Nazi officers and enlisted men and he had a Nazi flag, a helmet, a dagger and other things he took from them that he was shipping home. He also had a pistol, but wouldn't ship it at this time.

Bill House, who lived on Walnut Ridge, the ridge between Martins Mountain and Warrior Mountain, told me about his plan to start the Oldtown Boy Scout Troop Number 321. I told him that I was interested in becoming a scout and Bill informed me that there were now two of us in the troop. He gave me a small Boy Scout handbook and told me to learn the Tenderfoot requirements. Mom was glad that I was interested in scouting.

The first activity that Bill wanted the troop to take on was to man the Warrior mountain fire tower as much as possible. The tower was visible from our house on Martins Mountain. As a crow flies, I guess it would be about ten miles. I thought the tower duties could serve three purposes for me: I could use my Civil Air Patrol aircraft identification cards and spot any enemy aircraft approaching our area; I could be on the lookout for forest fires and report them; and I could be fulfilling my scouting "good deed" responsibilities.

On a Saturday morning I put on my military surplus utility belt that had attachment holes for a water canteen, first-aid kit, and scout knife. I carried my lunch bucket and bugle, because I wanted to show the bugle to Bill. I really had little idea of how long it would take me to hike off our mountain and along Walnut Ridge to Bill's place. He figured we could make it from his place to the fire tower by noon if I met him by nine. I didn't make it to Bill's until just before dinnertime, and after eating we set out and walked along the hollow between Walnut Ridge and Warrior Mountain until we came to the big power line, which provided a clear path up the side of Warrior Mountain. As we trudged along it occurred to me that it would have been much closer had I walked North from my house and then off Martins Mountain, using the clearing of this same power line. It would have saved me about half the distance. But it would have been all new territory for me and I had learned early on not to venture off alone in these mountains without the proper planning and preparation.

I was really tired and had to muster every ounce of strength in me to keep going up the side of Warrior Mountain, which was really steep, rocky and had a lot of brush. This area also had a bad reputation for rattlesnakes and copperheads; we saw and heard a few. In some places we were climbing hand over hand against the cliffs and rocks. When we reached the top of Warrior we had about two miles to hike along the ridge to the tower. We pulled down the bottom section of the ladder that led up the steel structure. I was so exhausted that I wasn't sure that I could trust my strength climbing up about 100 feet to the spotter platform. My legs and arms were burning when we reached the top and I had to rest on the floor for a while.

Bill had been checked out by a forest ranger on methods of using the plotting board, determining the location of a fire, and how to report it. We stayed there for a couple of hours and Bill taught me all he knew about the spotting job. The only smoke we saw was from home chimneys. Bill warned that I would have to be sure I was spotting a real forest fire before I reported it. Someone had reported smoke in the woods and it turned out to be a person making moonshine. That person was in a lot of trouble and the spotter feared for his life from the mountaineer's family.

The hike down was easier but my legs were about spent. The glamour of scouting was fading and I told Bill that I wasn't interested in committing to manning the fire tower, even though the Forest Department was short of manpower due to the war.

Bill signed my Scout book after he verbally tested me, and he made me a Tenderfoot Scout and presented me with a little gold Tenderfoot badge.

It was dark when I left Bill's house. I elected not to walk up the power line on Martins Mountain, a shortcut. Instead I continued on beyond the power line in Frog Hollow until I came to Mt. Tabor Church. The road to my house was the steepest at the church and by the graveyard. It was a pitch-black night and the only way for me to know that I was walking in the tire ruts and staying on the road was by the difference in the sounds of the gravel under my feet at each side of the rut. I was so tired that thoughts of ghosts coming out of the graveyard didn't even enter my mind, like they had at earlier times when I walked by here.

Soon, dim headlights were visible coming down the road; I recognized the sound of the loose fender squeaking on Dad's 1935 Ford pickup. Dad stopped the truck and said, "Where in the hell have you been?"

I told him and he couldn't believe that I took such a long hike. The muscles in my legs twitched and burned as I sat in the truck with my head back. I was totally exhausted. I told Dad, "Thanks for coming after me. I was considering making a bed of leaves and sleeping out—and by the way, you don't have to concern yourself about me going to the fire tower again."

Mom was so relieved when she heard about V-E Day. She was sure that her sons, Bill and Jesse, would be out of harm's way and coming home soon. Jesse was home within two months and we celebrated with him. He had a 30-day leave with orders to report to Fort Jackson, South Carolina. Bill wrote that his unit would remain in Austria until after the Allies had completed their occupation responsibilities.

When Jess wrote from Fort Jackson we couldn't believe what we were reading: his letter stated that the Army was preparing to send his unit to the Pacific War Zone, probably for the invasion of Japan. From the tone of this letter we knew that he believed his luck might run out and his odds were not good to make it through another stint of ground fighting. But V-J Day in August 1945 removed Mom's burden and the probability that Jesse would have to be in combat in Japan. He was discharged three months later at Fort Mead, Maryland.

Many things were happening. Servicemen were being discharged in droves, and they were allowed to wear their uniforms with a golden eagle patch sewn onto their left jacket pocket. Everyone referred to the patch as the "ruptured duck." So many changes were occurring in every area of our lives that the routine things at school and home were completely overshadowed by the war's end.

Mom nearly forgot that I was signed up for a two-week 4-H camp at Camp ALGAWA at Deep Creek Lake, Maryland. It was a former CCC camp and had great cabins, a mess hall and plenty of recreational facilities. The name ALGAWA was derived from the first two letters of the three Western Maryland counties that the kids came from: Allegheny, Garrett and Washington.

As we kids arrived at camp on school buses we were divided into three tribes—Chickasaw, Cherokee and Choctaw—and assigned to cabins by tribe. I was in the Chickasaw tribe and assigned to cabin number 5. We were issued bed sheets and a blanket and instructed to make our beds. We boys spoke hardly a word through this whole process. This was boring to me so I began introducing myself to the other guys and found out that we were all farm boys, and the most common thing that we had to talk about was farm animals and our pets. I had my Boy Scout knife and showed it around and then the guys began digging out their knives from their ditty bags and showing them.

Sometimes a guy is extremely lucky: Just before lights were put out the first night I saw a rat running along the lintel plate in the cabin. I opened the blade on my knife, told the guys to get out of the way, threw the knife, and pinned the rat to the ceiling. I finished off the rat and cleaned up my knife blade. The lights went out and in the dark a voice said, "Shipe, you sure are good throwing a knife."

I didn't say a word. My pride swelled to the point that I had to tell God, "Thank you, Lord, for your faithfulness. I could be the laughing stock of the cabin right now!"

The tribes were pitted against each other in team sports to win a camp trophy. The city boys were really good; some were members of the baseball team at their school and some were swimmers on the school team. The farm boys were from small schools where there weren't any organized sports so we were best at horseshoes, rifle marksmanship, shooting a bow and arrow, and the like. Our tribe tried hard to win the trophy but lost to the Choctaws, who rubbed it in with a song they sang, *The Mighty Choctaws.* The singing annoyed me. I had heard about "short-sheeting" bunks, and the guys in our tribe thought that was a neat idea. On the last day, during evening chow, we sneaked into the Choctaw cabins and short-sheeted their bunks. When the Choctaws were getting into bed we could hear them yelling about the sheets. The next morning we Chickasaws all whistled our Chickasaw tune as we loaded our gear on the bus and looked just guilty enough to ensure that the Choctaws knew who had done the trick.

Rumors said that we would have five or six new teachers at Oldtown School. Some would be GIs or wives of GIs returning to the area. The war years had changed our school. There was a lot of stress because the many substitutes were not able to maintain discipline and they didn't have the lessons as well planned as the regular teachers. The happy times at school had changed for both teachers and students. My grades were okay but I was not putting any extra effort into my schoolwork. I worried about how I would stack up against other kids in college entrance exams. The GI Bill was going to allow many older men to return to finish high school and colleges would be bursting with applicants over the next three or four years. Without good credentials my chances for scholarships would not be good.

Jesse announced that he had asked Emmadale Davis to marry him and their wedding would be real soon. The family was very happy for them, and since Jesse would be working for the Consolidated Orchard Company, it is possible that he and Emmadale would be able to move into the cottage next to us. Mom was really excited about having them as her neighbor. Dad, in his joking manner, said to Mom, "I'm not too sure that Emmadale will be as excited about living next door to her in-laws as you will be having them next door to you."

The major employers in the area, Celanese Company, Kelly Springfield Tire Company, and the B&O and Western Maryland railroads, were laying off a lot of employees. People were leaving the tri-state area to find work.

13

Foxfire

The Charles Atlas ads, showing a guy with cannonball biceps and a beautiful girl on his arm and kicking sand in the face of a skinny guy at the beach, began to catch my attention. The muscle-builder equipment being advertised seemed almost too simple to be true: a device with five interchangeable metal springs attached to handles at each end. The ad explained that with just a few minutes each day the user could look like famed weightlifter Charles Atlas and be a "sand kicker," just like in the picture.

I showed the ad to Mom and said, "A lot of the guys at school are beginning to get bigger biceps, and even though I'm working at the orchard and around the place every day my muscle development isn't what other guys are getting."

Mom laughed and said, "Don't worry about it. You're only fifteen. Look at Jesse, he was eighteen when he came home from basic training in the army and he had big biceps."

I continued to press the issue: "I don't believe I'm gonna develop like Jesse. I'm a much smaller-built guy. He's stocky like Dad. I think I'll be tall and lean like your brothers."

I allowed a few days to pass and then said, "I don't know anyone that uses the Charles Atlas muscle builder, but I'm sure it will work for me."

Mom replied, "You could probably get as much good out of fastening rubber car or bicycle inner tubes to the side of the barn and exercising your arm and chest muscles every day."

I said, "Yeah, I've also heard that if you pick up a baby calf the first day he is born and lift him every day thereafter, you could lift him as a steer. Could you ever imagine me lifting Johnnie Cake at the time she was butchered? She weighed over five hundred pounds!"

Mom looked at the ad and the price and said, "Okay, fill out the form and prepare an envelope for the order. Dad can get a money order tomorrow and you should have it in a couple of weeks."

Just as advertised, the Charles Atlas order came within two weeks. When I entered the kitchen there it was on the table where Dad had left it after going for the mail. Mom was curious enough to ask, "Are you going to open it now?"

I replied, "I'd better take it to my room. That way I'll have all the parts and papers there." I rushed upstairs, ripped open the box and examined my new prize. The muscle-builder had two red handles and five steel springs, each about one inch in diameter and about twice as long as screen door springs.

I began changing out of my school clothes into work clothes. Before putting on my shirt I took a good look at my bare physique in the mirror above my dresser and decided to give the equipment a try. I strained as hard as I could and couldn't spread the handles apart with all five springs attached. I removed the middle spring and even then I wasn't able to stretch the four remaining springs. So I removed all except two outer springs and then I was able to make it work. Thrusting my chest out, I began stretching the springs across my chest. I stretched them as far as my arms would reach, holding my breath, and I held my arms apart until I began to tremble. Then I relaxed and released the handles. As the spring coils collapsed they caught the skin on my chest and my right nipple was stuck in a coil. I wanted to scream from the pain. I had never had anything hurt as bad in all my born days. I had to stretch the handles apart to rescue my body part from the grasp of the thing. I threw the darned contraption onto my bed and was sorry I had ever wanted it.

Closely examining my chest I could see red marks where the coils pinched my skin. My right tit, which hurt the worst, had a big blue blood blister on the nipple.

Mom opened the downstairs door and yelled, "Are you going to let me see the Charles Atlas thing?"

I began slipping on my shirt and answered, "Okay, I'll be right down." I had to make a quick plan because I wasn't going to repeat what had just happened. I picked the thing off the bed and applied a third spring to the middle of the handles to make sure it looked really tough for Mom's demonstration.

Downstairs, Mom said, "Let me see it." She held the muscle builder and admired how simple it was and said that she couldn't figure why they charged so much for it. She said she was proud that I was already able to use it with three springs. I kept mum.

Mom said, "Well, are you going to show me how it works?"

I replied, "This can be used on muscle groups other than arms, back and chest. I'll show you how it works on leg muscles." I placed the toe of my right shoe in one handle, then with both hands I began to stretch the springs upward as far as I could. My arms began to tremble and shake and then, without warning the handle slipped off my foot. It whizzed within a fraction of an inch of my nose and slammed into the ceiling.

Mom yelled, "Whoops! Plumb my soul to goodness! You've scared the daylights out of me! Oh my soul, look at the big hole you've put in my new kitchen ceiling!"

I was speechless. I looked at the ceiling. The red paint from the handle had left its mark and caused the hole to appear much larger.

I told Mom how hard I was going to work to make enough money to fix the hole in the acoustic ceiling tile.

Mom said, "Maybe you should keep that thing at the barn. Its dangerous to use around the house."

I said, "That's a good idea—and your idea about using rubber inner tubes was a good one too."

When Dad saw the hole in the ceiling he commented, "The best muscle-building equipment is to wrap your hands around the handles of pitchforks, axes, plows, shovels and the like and your muscles will grow. And by-the-by, the stable needs a good cleaning right now."

I gathered up my Charles Atlas stuff and headed for the barn, and from that day I did all of my muscle-building activity at the barn.

Jesse and Emmadale were married, and they settled into the cottage next to our home. The wedding was small, and after their honeymoon a good story surfaced: Jesse had picked up his suit at the cleaners and rushed home to get dressed in order to make it to the ceremony on time. As he began putting on his trousers he wasn't able to put his legs through his pants. Someone had sewn his pant legs shut. Mom was upset that someone would do such a terrible trick at such an important time. Jesse was a little late for his wedding. The culprit was never identified.

One thing the mountains in Western Maryland could be counted on was good snow for sledding and toboganing. Local kids gathered on a hill between the Spring Gap Post Office and the Reckley's place just off Twiggtown Road. The guys and girls gathered wood for a huge bonfire. If the moon was near full we had ideal conditions to ride down the hills. We used cardboard to make toboggans—not real toboggans, but that's what we called our devices. Often we slid down the hill totally out of control. Sometimes we could fit four kids on a large sheet of cardboard that came from a box such as a refrigerator carton. If the front person could lift the front edge of the cardboard we had a great machine to head down the hill. We'd go at high speed, rotating as we slid. Sometimes we ended up going down backward. We had to hold tight to each other to stay on the cardboard. Each of the guys would maneuver to have their favorite girl ride in front so that we could squeeze the dickens out of them. Every ride ended with kids piled in a heap and covered with snow.

We had to trudge back up the hill in knee-deep snow. The laughing and yelling at each other could be heard echoing off the walls of the hollow along Twigtown road. The yelling intensified when someone would let a snowball fly and war broke out. When we reached the top of the hill we were covered with snow. We all crowded close to the fire to get warm. Often our clothing became so hot that steam rose from our garments. When someone got too close to the fire and his or her clothing would singe; the odor smelled like burning hair. As soon as someone smelled that odor, he'd yell a warning:" Someone is burning!" and we would check each other's backside for fire.

Ice-skating on the Old Chesapeake and Ohio Canal near Lock House 72 was another opportunity to gather and have fun. We built bonfires on the bank of the canal just below the curve on Route 51—called "Deadman's Curve" because so many accidents occurred there. A group of kids would gather at dark and skate for two or three hours on weekends, and on some school nights if the word got out that the ice was really hard.

Kenneth and I found a couple pairs of clamp-on skates hanging on the side of the corncrib wall, so we cleaned them and oiled the rusty parts. Dad sharpened the blades, using a honing technique that produced two good edges. The skates required a key to tighten the clamps to our shoes. We couldn't find a skate key so we carried pliers to use in tightening the clamps. Our work shoes worked best, providing a sturdy sole for tightening the clamps onto. We also wore heavy socks. Even with the clamps twisted so tight that the sole of our work shoes buckled, the skates would come off. Playing tin-can hockey or tag became difficult because losing a skate going fast put you flat on your butt or worse, face-first onto the ice.

As we walked up the mountain Kenneth and I had long discussions about whether it was worth the hike down the mountain and back up in the dark on cold nights, in order to join our friends to go tobogganing or skating. We admitted to each other that girls being present might have been the deciding factor in our decision to walk off the mountain. We talked about what a guy had to do to have a real date and concluded that a date had to have an invitation, an acceptance by the girl, an activity, and an ending; and that the guy was totally responsible for safety and security that met the parent's approval.

"With a set of requirements like this, tobogganing and skating certainly were not official dates," I maintained.

Kenneth replied, "It doesn't come close to a date, you dummy!"

"The fun I have hugging the girls on the cardboard slides make it seem like a date, and I don't get teased about going steady and all that stuff."

"You have to let the teasing be like water running off a duck's back," he said. "The feathers protect the duck and water never gets to his skin."

"I can handle most of it, but I hate it when the guy's sing, 'First comes love and then comes marriage, here comes Ken pushing a baby carriage,' That makes me so mad I'd really like to clean their plows!"

Kenneth laughed. "You just have to learn how to take it. And besides, many of the Spring Gap girls have two or three brothers and you don't want to do anything dumb like punch out a brother, 'cuz you'd have the brothers and the girl cleaning *your* plow."

"You know, dating around here has a certain draw to it, but it also has a whole lot of drawbacks."

"What do you mean?"

"Hugging and squeezing the girls has a certain draw for me, if you know what I mean." I couldn't see Kenneth's face in the dark; however, I knew him well enough to know that he was smiling as he gave a half-laughing reply, "I know what you mean."

The change of seasons from winter to spring resolved the question of whether we would go skating or tobogganing. The constant below-freezing temperatures were generally over in February. Folks had a saying, if March comes in like a lion it will go out like a lamb, and vice-versa.

The arrival of spring on Martins Mountain was something to behold. The first clue that a major event was about to occur was the arrival of large trucks filled with beehives. The hives were set out along the perimeter of the orchard.

I knew that sap was rising in the apple trees when the bark on the trees turned from a ghostly gray to a greenish hue and the buds began to swell. The nose peeking out from the bud appeared pink at first; then it would open to show its full beauty, all this occurring before the leaves were out.

Many people drove to the mountain during blossom time. The cars moved slowly along the orchard roads as the occupants tried hard to absorb the beauty and aroma. We mountain people who lived in this beauty spring after spring were caught off guard when folks from elsewhere asked us to explain what the apple blossoms meant to us. To put into words what it was like to live in the middle of a blanket of apple blossoms that stretched five miles was beyond our descriptive ability. I once attempted to quantify the experience, based on the assumption that the trees produced 100,000 bushels of prime apples each year. Each bushel contained about 65 apples and only about one blossom in ten would make it to maturity after the thinning process. From this analysis, visitors to the mountain were enjoying about 65 million blossoms.

Pulling weeds from the garden and feeding them to the hogs became a pleasure for me. I enjoyed feeding them to Lady, who was maturing very fast. I was getting excited about showing her at the Allegany County Fair, scheduled for August. Kenneth and I were going to be able to spend two nights and three days living in the swine pavilion.

The work on the orchard was difficult now that I was able to work every position in the spray crews. Dragging two hundred feet of hose up and down the sides of the mountain behind the spray gunner was hot, tiring work. Spraying the trees to ward off insects was an endless summer job. Sometimes the gunner would exchange places with me so he could rest his arms. The high pressure of the nozzle required constant arm tension and you had to keep the spray gun in constant motion. The orchard foreman, Turk, was continually checking the trees to be sure that the leaves were wetted on both the top and bottom.

Young apple trees were planted now on the old Millholland place, making the Consolidated Orchard trees continuous from the power line on the south end of the mountain to the high power line on the north, a good five miles. The conversion of our farm to orchard was complete. The landscape held no resemblance to the farm and the original orchards, where Dad and my family worked for six years eking out a living and attempting to make sharecropping profitable.

I daydreamed a lot about the future as I worked, trying to figure out what to do after graduation from high school. I knew that I needed money to get a college education. I was absolutely convinced that hard work, ambition, and aggressiveness would allow me to reach my goals. I also thought about marriage and things like that. I thought I would marry a local girl and somehow live happily ever after; that was the model most guys in these parts followed.

Kenneth and I were ready to load the pig crate into the back of Dad's pickup. We had two choices: We could load Lady into the crate and lift the crate onto the truck, or position the truck against a bank and walk Lady into the crate on the truck. Lady was too heavy for us to lift so the decision was to coax and herd her to where the truck was parked and into the crate. To Dad's amazement and ours, Lady went straight away into the crate.

The 4-H and Future Farmers of America swine pavilion at the fairgrounds was busy like a beehive. Boys were unloading their pigs, which had to be poked and prodded from their crates into the strange surroundings. The animals were squealing and making a big fuss, then cautiously sniffing every inch of the walkway to their assigned pen. The boys had a winning swagger in their walk.

Kenneth found a gate and I opened the crate for Lady to come out. We herded her down the aisle between the pens to the far end, where the Hampshire hogs were housed. Lady stopped near a pen in the Poland China hog section and took a healthy leak. The stream ran into one of the pens where a kid from Garrett County had his white Poland China pig and the kid became all huffy. I gave him a grin and when Lady was through I tapped her on the rump and we continued down the aisle to her pen. Kenneth was spreading straw and claiming the space where he was going to sleep in the pen that adjoined Lady's. His selection left me sleeping against the boards that separated the pens.

We closed the tailgate on the pickup. Dad wasn't anywhere in sight. We located him at the dairy cattle barn, enjoying himself, and he walked with us back to where we were going to sleep. He chuckled at the idea of sleeping next to Lady then bid us goodbye. As he started to drive away he stuck his head out the truck window and said, "Sure hope your snoring doesn't keep Lady awake all night. Ha, Ha, Ha!"

Kenneth and I reported to the office, where we picked up the schedule of events and our exhibitor credentials. A quick review of the schedule revealed that Hampshire hogs would not be shown until the second day. Mom had packed us plenty of good food for supper so we washed up at a water spigot, sat on a bale of straw, and ate.

As the sun set the hot August day was cooling some and we could see the bright lights from the carnival midway on the other side of the racetrack. The Ferris wheel was all lit up, and we headed directly for it. The glare of the midway lights made us squint. Crowds were starting to arrive and the sideshow barkers were yelling about how great their show was. They had to yell louder than the music being played for the hoochiecoochie dancers. Before we got to the Ferris wheel, I excitedly coaxed Kenneth to see one show—the half-woman, half-reptile. We entered the dimly lit tent that housed the creature. It was so spooky that I only gave a glance at something in a pit. We didn't hang around long enough to figure out whether it was real or not; our immediate conclusion was that it probably was phony. We each had wasted 50 cents.

We enjoyed the rides. We stuffed ourselves with hot dogs and cotton candy. We tried without success to knock down bottles at a tent that promised a prize every time whether we knocked down any or not; we got a prize all right, but it wasn't worth much—nothing like the large stuffed animals hanging around the tent.

Next morning we awoke to the sounds of the cows, sheep and horses calling out, wanting to return to their homes. I fed Lady and we high-tailed it over to the judging pavilion. To our surprise, the hogs were all scrubbed clean and their coats glistened in the morning sun. They even had their toenails shined. Kenneth looked at me and said, "We have some work to do to spruce Lady up!"

We waited our turn at the place to wash pigs and as we began to scrub Lady's tummy, she flopped down with a big pig smile. We scrubbed her until her skin was pink. I noticed that some other boys had wiped their pigs with a rag that had motor oil on it. I used an oily rag that was hanging on the fence and the oil wipe did the trick: Lady's bristles took on new life and she glistened and sparkled as she moved.

My 4-H and FFA teacher, Mr. House, had entered me in a contest to judge vegetables, field corn, chickens and beef cattle. The vegetables and animals had been pre-judged by senior judges; each contestant's scorecards were compared with the experts' and scored. I received a first-place ribbon for chicken judging and a third-place ribbon for corn. Teachers received pennants for later presentation when school was in session.

It was time to show Lady. Kenneth pinned a Number 4 to my back and opened the pen. I used a small hickory stick to lightly tap Lady on the rump, keeping her going down the long aisle to the judging pavilion. My mind began to swarm with apprehensive thoughts: I worried about how Lady looked, and how she might behave. Some of the hogs did fine until they got to the ring and then, without warning, they turned around, running at full speed, and the kids could never get them back for judging.

Lady slowly meandered toward the show ring, nose down and grunting with each step as she sniffed the ground. There were six pigs in the ring and the judges eyed them as we walked in a circle. The judges walked around behind us. Some squatted down to peer across the backs of the animals. They were writing on clipboards. I saw that Kenneth was sitting on the front row of the spectators' section. He raised his hands and showed me he had both fingers crossed.

When the judging was over a male official and a young woman came into the ring. She wore a sash that read, "Miss 4H 1947" and held three large ribbons in her hands—blue, red and white. The gentleman announced the third-place winner, and the girl presented the white ribbon to a kid. The second-place winner was announced and the kid right next to me received the red ribbon. When the first-place winner was announced I thought I heard number five had won—but the cute girl walked toward me and gave me the blue ribbon with a smile. I felt my face flush and I knew I was blushing. Kenneth was going nuts in the stands. It was over. Gladheart Lady Olive's Best, was a blue-ribbon champion.

Kenneth helped me get Lady settled back in her pen and I hung the blue ribbon on the gate. Kenneth climbed into the pen to give Lady a big hug. She squealed and swung her head back and forth real hard, tossing Kenneth against the wall of the pen. I told him: "Pigs hate to be hugged. I think they believe you're going to strangle them."

It was raining again at the fairgrounds. Kenneth said, "I sure wish it would stop. I'd like to go back to see the midway tonight."

I answered, "I don't think we should go back, even if it stops raining. Those places just take our money."

Kenneth dug a deck of cards from his bag and we started playing knock gin rummy. The heat and humidity were really bad and it continued to rain. About midnight we had a terrible electrical storm with a lot of thunder and lightening. We didn't sleep much that night.

We were up and ready for Dad to take us home, and he arrived just before noon. When we got home Mom met us as we got out of the truck. I handed her the blue ribbon and she told me she was very proud of the way I'd showed Lady at the fair and won first place. She added, "By the way, your paychecks for the last two weeks' work at the orchard are on the table."

I said, "Okay, we are going to walk down to the Millstone and cash our checks. We should be home before ten."

At the Millstone store, Erma, the owner, cashed our checks and wanted to hear all about our experience showing my pig. We gave her a short version. The barroom part of the store was separated from the grocery part by an imaginary line at the end of the meat counter and the folks in the the barroom part were all ears when we told about sleeping with a pig at the fair. They erupted in laughter and announced that they needed another round of beer after hearing such a blue-ribbon story. We finished drinking our tonic and eating some cheese crackers and didn't stick around the store very long before we headed home.

I said, "We really made a mistake telling about sleeping at the pig pen. I'm sure they understood, but now they have a good story to tell on us."

Kenneth replied, "Sure is strange how some folk like to twist things around. They will only remember that we slept with a pig."

As we walked up the mountain road it became dark and foggy. The trees were dripping water from their leaves as the dew collected on them. Just before we reached the high power line, Kenneth said, "Look at that glow in the woods!"

I answered, "Yea, that's really a weird light." We were both straining our eyes looking over the road bank and into the woods.

Kenneth used his foot to feel around on the ground for a rock and when he found one he threw it into the woods. The rock hit a tree with a loud crack and water drops came showering down.

I yelled, "Oh my God, here it comes after us!"

Kenneth jumped on my back, yelling, "Run, run!"

I screamed, "Get off me! Let's get the hell out of here!"

We ran the mile home without stopping. Mom and Dad were in the living room, reading newspapers as we stumbled into the house. Mom took one look at us and said, "What in Heaven's name has happened?"

Kenneth, gasping for breath, blurted out: "We saw this huge thing that was full of light in the woods and it came crashing through the woods after us and it chased us all the way home!"

Dad looked at me, then said: "Now wait a minute, did you see a light or did something come out of the woods after you?"

Kenneth said, "I threw a rock at the light and the thing came after us!"

I told Dad, "I didn't see him throw the rock. Maybe that made the water fall from the trees and we just thought something was coming after us."

Dad said, "Let's get in the pickup and we'll drive down there and take a look."

Kenneth said, "I'll stay here with Pearlzie, okay?"

I said, "I'm taking a shotgun with us 'cuz I believe we might have to use it."

Dad replied with a frown, "No, we don't need a gun and it's never a good idea to have a loaded gun with you in the dark."

In the truck, Dad said to me, "I believe I know what this is, but let me investigate first. Don't worry, everything will be okay."

When we got near the spot I said, "Go slow, it's real near here. This is the place! See the bags of stuff we dropped when we started running." Dad stopped the truck, turned off the headlights, got out of the truck and climbed the road bank. I opened the door and stood on the running board, peering into the woods.

Dad called out, "Yeah, just what I thought—its foxfire. Come here and take a look!"

I joined him, walking cautiously about 25 feet into the woods. There was a bright glow coming from an old log.

Dad said, "I've heard about foxfire all my born days, but this is the first time I have seen it with my own eyes. Weather conditions and the decay process of a log have to be perfect for the phosphorus in certain wood to glow like this."

When we got back to the house, Mom was relieved but Kenneth didn't want to hear about foxfire. He said, "I have this clear vision of a monster romping out of the woods and chasing us home. I even felt his hot breath on the back of my neck as we ran. That is the last time I'll walk the mountain in the dark."

Dad said, "You boys aren't the first to have the daylights scared out them by foxfire. You now have a story to tell that few will understand and most won't believe."

The Spring Gap boys had finished working their last full week at the orchard for the summer. We were all happy to head back to school and were relieved that we would only be working on Saturdays.

Mrs. Gilbert Miller had driven her car into our driveway, and she and Mom had been talking for an unusually long time. Mom came into the kitchen where I was and said, "Mrs. Miller wants to talk to you about something that is very important. After you have heard what she is saying, then you have to decide. The decision is totally up to you; if you want to do what she proposes it is okay with me."

I looked at Mom and said, "Come on, now what have I done?"

Mom replied, "You haven't done anything, she wants to talk to you about an opportunity for you."

As I approached the car Mrs. Miller got out and said, "Kenneth, I will be driving each morning and evening down to the school bus stop at Spring Gap. My boys, Harry and Bernie, will be attending Pennsylvania Avenue School in Cumberland and the same bus continues to Fort Hill High. I know you're looking for every opportunity to improve your education. I believe Fort Hill High offers a greater variety of courses than Oldtown School. I have room in my car for an additional person and I'm offering it to you."

I looked at her, then replied, "I respect your opinion. I've heard that Fort Hill offers diplomas other than general. I'd really like to have an academic diploma. That should improve my chances of getting into college."

Mrs. Miller looked me in the eyes and said, "It isn't absolutely necessary for you to have a foreign language or an academic diploma to enter college. What is important is that you take strong academic courses. You'll have to pass an entrance examination."

I scratched my head, kicked a few stones with my foot and said, "Okay, what time should I be beside the road Monday morning?"

"Seven o'clock," she replied.

I blurted out quickly, "Thank you very much. I'll be by the road on Monday."

Running toward the house to tell Mom about my decision, it occurred to me that I wouldn't be riding off the mountain in Mr. Mumaw's car with Kenneth and Herbie. And I wouldn't be seeing my classmates each school day at Oldtown School. I perked up when I remembered that Fort Hill High offered a course in aeronautics, which was what I wanted to learn.

Mrs. Miller pulled her car off Highway 51 at the bus stop at Spring Gap and as I got out I was surprised to see two of my classmates from Oldtown School, Norma Lee and Barbara Jean. They also were changing schools in order to take commercial courses at Fort Hill High, courses that weren't offered at Oldtown.

Registering at Fort Hill, I felt like I was at the A&P Supermarket with all the course choices to make. After I completed my schedule I noted one glaring error: I had no study periods.

When I reported to gym class Coach Cavanaugh wouldn't let me participate because I didn't have gym clothes and a towel. When I got home and told Mom I needed a gym suit and towel she remarked, "What is this world coming to! Now kids need a special suit just for play."

The fall season around home was nothing like it used to be before the farm was converted to an orchard. Harvesting was confined to what we grew in Mom's garden patch. She insisted that we cut the sweet corn stalks and stack them into shocks so that she could place her pumpkins around them. Mom missed seeing the large cornfields filled with shocks.

Harvest time got us boys to start thinking about tricks. A few of the Spring Gap boys, including Kenneth and me, planned a visit to Oldtown to perform some Halloween pranks. Hartley drove his father's car and his brother Bill, Kenneth and I rode with him, anticipating mischief. We planned to upset as many outhouses as we could and then skidaddle back to Spring Gap without getting caught.

The first outhouse had a dog in it. As we started tipping the toilet, the dog began barking and a porch light came on. We gave a final shove and over it went, with the dog yelping inside. We ran real fast and stopped behind a clump of trees. The adrenaline had my heart beating ninety to nothing as I hid behind a bush, watching to see if the outhouse owner was going to follow us. He didn't. We continued our tipping at a few more outhouses. We knew of a double-seated model that belonged to one of the teachers at Oldtown School. It took every bit of our combined strength to tip the big privvy but eventually it went over and fell with a terrific crash. The owners' porch lights come on, as did two or three of his neighbors' lights, and a shotgun blasted. I heard the shot zipping through the leaves over my head and I ran up a hill in the dark and found myself in mid-air, then sliding down the bank of the Western Maryland Railroad cut. Shale gravel came pouring down from the side of the bank as all four of us landed near the tracks. Both of my ankles were hurting like mad, but we raced down the tracks to where we had parked the car near the school. We climbed in and sped off toward Paw Paw. We hoped to make it appear that guys from over the river in West Virginia had done the dastardly deeds. Hartley turned the car around at the Town Crick Bridge and drove us back to Spring Gap. We had plenty of scratches and bruises to remember this night.

A Halloween prank that Dad taught me was to take a long length of sewing thread and attach it to a thumbtack and press the thumbtack into the wood of a windowpane. The idea was to stand off a distance from the window and rub the thread with a piece of resin. Rubbing the thread with the resin made the whole window vibrate and caused an eerie sound. Dad and I agreed that I should try the trick on my sister Georgia when she was in the bedroom alone. The trick worked well, for I only had to draw the resin across the thread a couple of times before Georgia came screaming out of the bedroom into the living room. I saw Dad through the living room window, laughing until he had to remove his glasses to wipe tears from his eyes. Mom didn't like it at all. She let me have it when I came inside. Dad and I both stopped laughing. Mom looked at Dad with suspicion. He continued reading his paper and I went up to bed.

Kenneth joined the Marine Corps in December 1947 and reported to Paris Island, South Carolina to attend boot camp. He wrote a letter telling us he was sorry he didn't come to say goodbye before he left. He didn't because he was sure Mom would do all she could to change his mind and tell him that he should finish high school. He wrote about some of his experiences at boot camp and said he was looking forward to coming home on leave in April.

While I was eating breakfast, Mom asked, "How are you doing in school? I notice that you are spending a lot of time studying at night."

I replied, "I'm enjoying school, but I didn't realize how much of a load I've taken on. Chemistry, algebra, aeronautics, English and world history are subjects that require a lot of extra study, and the shop and drafting courses also require a lot of work. I'll just have to buckle down more and make sure I do well."

Mom asked, "Is there anything that I can do to help?"

I answered, "Not really, except maybe you could get someone to pick up an application for my driver's license. I can't believe that I'll be sixteen in one week. I'm living out the saying, 'Sweet sixteen and never been kissed.'"

Mom replied, "Now, don't you worry about the kissing stuff. All that will come in due time."

One evening I was walking on Baltimore Street in Cumberland and I noticed a small crowd gathered around some Marines. They had a banner asking for men to join the U.S. Marine Corps Reserve. One of the Marines motioned for me to come near and asked, "Why don't you walk over to the Armory tonight and see what's going on?"

I asked, "What are the hours?"

He replied, "We meet every Wednesday night from six to ten. Why don't you walk down there now and see what's going on?"

The Armory was a couple blocks off Baltimore Street near the Southern States Cooperative feed store. I entered and, there on the gymnasium floor, guys were disassembling and re-assembling rifles, machine guns, pistols and mortars. A uniformed staff sergeant greeted me, saying, "Hi, my name is Jack Lee, what's yours?"

I replied, "I'm Ken Shipe. A Marine uptown told me to come by and see what's going on."

Sergeant Lee said, "We are forming up a new company of Marine reserves here in Cumberland. What grade are you in?"

I replied, "I'm a junior at Fort Hill High School."

The sergeant replied, "We have quite a few Fort Hill High School men in our unit. We get a full day's pay for only four hours of drill each week. Let me give you a parental permission form to take home. If you come back next Wednesday with your form signed by one of your parents we will have medical personnel here, and when you pass the medical you will be sworn in. How about it?"

I replied, "Let me think about it."

When I climbed into the back of Dad's pickup at the feed store the sights and sounds at the Armory filled my head. I thought how good it was to be needed and how Sergeant Lee thought I was seventeen years old—old enough to join simply because I was a junior.

When we arrived home I went upstairs and laid the parental permission form on my dresser. I had to force myself to realize that there wasn't any way for me to join the reserves. I took a detailed look at the form; it required my name, date of birth and a parent's signature.

What I saw in the armory was so inviting to me that I couldn't get being a Marine out of my mind. I had to figure a way. I knew neither Mom nor Dad would sign the form.

I only practiced signing Mom's signature three times. I filled out the form using 1931 as my birth year. (I was born in 1932.)

On April 1, 1948, I took my medical examination and was sworn into the Marines as a private. My orange identity card had my serial number 1040888 and indicated the period of enlistment as "INDEF." Sergeant Lee took me out on the Armory floor and introduced me to the guys in the 60 mm mortar platoon. Sergeant Shade, one of the squad leaders, lived in Oldtown and I arranged to ride to drill each Wednesday with him.

When I got home Mom and Dad were settling down for the evening and I asked to speak to them about a decision I had made. I announced that I had joined a military reserve unit in Cumberland. I portrayed the Marine unit as a type of auxiliary and the next logical step beyond Boy Scouts.

Mom asked, "What do you have to do?"

I replied, "It requires a four-hour drill each Wednesday night at the Armory and attending summer camp for two weeks each year. I'll be riding with Sergeant Shade from Oldtown to the drills each Wednesday evening."

Dad asked, "Will he bring you up the mountain?"

I said, "I'm planning on walking the mountain. Its a little much to expect him to drive up here."

Dad looked up from his newspaper and directly into my eyes and said, "Don't expect me to take on the job of meeting you at the Millstone at that late hour."

I replied, "I understand. I took on this obligation and I'll figure out how to make it to the meetings and back."

Riding back and forth to school each day with Mrs. Miller and her boys was a challenging time for me, for Mrs. Miller loved to talk about issues. I knew that she was a well-known, well-respected lady activist and a member of some influential organizations in Cumberland, as well as a leader of the Spring Gap Ladies Auxiliary. In fact, if I had realized it, I very well could have been riding daily with one of the most influential individuals in our parts. Mrs. Miller loved to discuss current events and had a way of getting me to express my opinion on issues. If I didn't have an opinion she would talk about the issue until I formed one. I learned many things from her and it wasn't long until I knew where she stood on current issues. For example, we both loved animals and believed in game management. Yet, she knew I loved to hunt and I knew she hated hunting as a method of wildlife management. We both agreed on the need for soil conservation, but she was opposed to the cutting of forests for lumber and cultivation. I believed that it was prudent to cut trees for wood products and to farm the land for profit as long as the farmer observed anti-erosion and crop rotation techniques. I really appreciated Mrs. Miller. Even though I was a captive audience in her car, she never made me feel like a prisoner. She never preached, probed or questioned me about dating, or asked me whom I liked or disliked. She never gossiped about neighbors or asked me about my observations of the behavior of others. She never discussed the business aspects of the Consolidated Orchard Company or the influences that her husband, Gilbert, whom she called Gib, could make as an owner and officer of this large company. I believed that after Mom, Mrs. Miller was the woman that had my best interest in mind.

One afternoon while we were riding up the mountain, Mrs. Miller posed a question: "Kenneth, with the full plate of schoolwork, Saturday work on the orchard and your church activities, why in the world did you join the Marine Reserves and take on more responsibility?"

I sat quietly for a few seconds. I knew I had to give a reply that would withstand debate, so I answered, "Simply put, they said that they wanted me and I believe their cause is worthy. It fulfills my response to the call of my country."

Beyond that, I told her, I had decided I was now making choices that would steer my destiny. My parents had given me a wonderful, healthy and happy home life and I believed their vision for me was something beyond working in the soil as a sharecropper.

I said I didn't have a model to follow or a set of steps laid out in some book to lead me; therefore, I was allowing my own intuition to guide me. I noted that I'd graduate in a little over a year and I refused to allow events to overtake me. I'd always be preparing for the future and have my action plan. I would not be following career paths or grooves well traveled, like the grooves on a worn out and scratchy phonograph record.

She glanced at me with a surprised look and said, "I'm concerned that you're taking on too much. I don't want you to become disenchanted with what you're doing and lose sight of the great opportunities that lie ahead for you. I believe you need to allow yourself more time to evaluate and weigh what is critical in making decisions to meet your goals. I believe you are trying to do too much."

I replied, "I appreciate your concern. I can handle the hard work. Its in my genes." And I said I was prepared to make whatever choices it takes to enable me to leave the mountain and support myself immediately after graduation. Being a Marine was one of many options. "Do you know what I mean?" I asked.

Mrs. Miller answered, "I know what you mean."

Hunting season in Western Maryland was a special time but this year was more special than ever, for the Consolidated Orchard Company was going to allow deer hunting on its property, which had previously been posted with "no hunting allowed" signs. The deer herds had grown so large that they were eating buds from the apple trees and killing many of the small trees that had been planted on the Millholland place.

I had my rifle when I reported to the work camp at the appointed time of 4 a.m. to meet the dozen orchard workers who were waiting to take positions for the hunt. In these parts one form of hunting was to drive the deer into areas where hunters were stationed along well-traveled deer trails in standing positions: the drive and stand method form of hunting.

Mr. Gilbert Miller was in charge of the hunt. As soon as I arrived the hunters began to form into two groups, drivers and stationary standers. Mr. Miller said, "Kenneth, Mr. Parks, the oldest member of the crew, won't be on the first drive for he isn't feeling well. Since you are the youngest member, I want you to take his place in a stationary stand just below the spray pump house and along the woods." He loaded those of us who would be standers into his Jeep and drove us toward the northern end of the orchard.

It was dark when I climbed out of the Jeep. I had to walk in front of it to load shells into my .30–06 caliber rifle by the light of the headlamps. Just at sunrise I could hear the men start the drive along the east side of the mountain. I was positioned on a bank beside an easily recognizable deer trail. Within minutes I heard a deer trotting just to my right and coming toward me. I had to squint to see it in the early light. Then a large buck jumped into the road within 10 feet of me. I raised my rifle and fired. The flash momentarily blinded me. I reloaded and held the rifle on the animal lying motionless in the middle of the road until I verified that it was dead. I counted the points on the rack and both sides added up to 14, a real dandy of a deer.

Being successful on a hunt was a sure way to gain acceptance and respect of the hunters and my peers. Also, the newspaper printed the name of the hunter, the weight and number of antler points of the kill.

Consolidated Orchard Company special deer hunt. I'm far right with
14-point white tail—1948

I was experiencing a situation where I felt like I was straddling two cultural views: one, the things we did to survive from the land on the mountain which I accepted as normal and the other was from people who viewed our mountain ways as abnormal, even cruel, crude or foreign. I was weary of defending my mountain ways and the need to take stands of justification of issues and positions that came natural to me because of my being reared in a mountain environment.

My greatest concern about hunting and killing a deer was the possible rebuke that I would receive from Mrs. Miller the next morning in her car on the way to school. The food value of the hunt was about 30 pounds of venison for each hunter. But the true reason that I joined the hunt was the opportunity to win instant acceptance by the hunters and the bragging rights of a successful marksman. Acceptance by the hunters outweighed the rebuke I expected when Mrs. Miller heard about my kill. I was sure she would not agree with my reason for joining the hunting crew, but I felt safe because I had an avenue of escape—her husband led the hunt. She never mentioned the deer hunt to me.

14

Finding my own way

Springtime is magical in the Allegheny Mountains. On Martins Mountain everything that had been dormant during the winter was struggling to come alive and to do whatever its life force required of it to ensure its existence. The plants and trees emerging from the ground, the wild animals giving birth and nurturing their young, made me feel that everything on the mountain except the rocks was engaged in a struggle to live. Insects were especially interesting. I spent hours watching an ant carrying leaves and other bits of material to improve an anthill after the winter. I studied the praying mantis; I would speak to one and observe how it would tilt its head and look at me, as though it heard me and was responding to my voice. I observed a fawn as it wobbled around on its spindly legs minutes after being born. Martins Mountain is a good place to observe the changes of the seasons.

One species of mushroom that remains a mystery to me is the morel. Folks who know about morels either love or hate the dark-brown, spongy, conical-shaped delicacy. People in the Spring Gap area lust after morels and they scheme all winter to decide where and when to start searching for one of the first foods that can be harvested in spring. The morels were difficult to find—so difficult that people who found them would not think of marketing them. Here on the mountain if you gathered three or four messes of morels each spring you were considered very fortunate. I dream of one day figuring out how to grow these mushrooms and market them; their value can be compared to truffles and they may be even more valuable.

Dad was absolutely convinced that the morels grew only under apple trees. He believed the decayed apples were the source of the spores that seeded the growth of morels. I challenged him often because every now and then I had found a morel on the bank of the road where there wasn't an apple tree within hundreds of yards. He defended his theory by allowing that birds probably carried the spore to that spot. Other folks claimed they had found the tasty morsels under poplar trees, miles away from apple trees. Dad dismissed these stories as misleading myths.

Much has been written about people who lust after the morels, people who are like cultists, following the spring sun northward, beginning in the Carolinas and ending in Canada; with the sole purpose of gathering morels from the woodlands. American Indians also valued the morel mushroom, for they would thread the morels onto a string, dry and store them for winter food. Dried morels soaked in water, absorbs water and it returns to its original shape and taste.

At our house the ritual of hunting morels began when a family member was spotted heading out toward one of the apple orchards carrying an empty cellophane bread wrapper to be used as a bag to hold the mushrooms. Morels are usually hunted alone, for the location of a good spot is held secret and you can claim bragging rights as the best mushroom hunter, knowing many locations. Mushroom hunters have been known to give false information as to location, time of day, temperature, relative humidity, day of the week, phase of the moon and other factors.

Any person in our family who found mushrooms was expected to bring them home and clean them. Mom happily cooked them into an egg omelet that was served with country ham. The whole family enjoyed the feast. The mushroom season ended about the time the apple trees were in full bloom.

I was proud when I heard someone refer to me as a high school senior. I had been happy to make it through my junior year. Even though I didn't make the grades that I wanted, being able to change from one high school to another, carry extra credits, and be accepted by my classmates at Fort Hill was an important accomplishment. I had a checklist of things I wanted to achieve as a senior: attend the senior prom, apply for any college scholarship opportunities, and, maybe, have a steady girlfriend. Going steady was a path that many guys and gals were following, and some were talking about getting married right after graduation. But getting married was something I wasn't prepared to think about yet.

The major event for the summer was to attend two-week maneuvers with my Marine unit at Camp Lejeune, North Carolina. Some of the guys at the orchard and around Spring Gap teased me that the heat in North Carolina in late June and early July coupled with the tough infantry training would make me sorry I ever joined the Marine Reserves.

The time arrived, June 1948, for USMCR Company D, 5th Infantry Battalion, to depart for Camp Lejeune. The unit consisted of three rifle platoons, one machine gun platoon, one 60mm-mortar platoon, and a headquarters platoon. Our company commander brought the unit to attention at the Cumberland Armory and we marched to Baltimore Street and crossed the B&O tracks to the Queen City Railroad Station. We were in full battle dress, with weapons, packs, helmets and canvas leggings. I thought we looked good and sounded better as the 150 male voices called out marching cadence and the choruses echoed from the buildings. Our looks bore little relation to our experience because in my mortar platoon of 21 men, only Staff Sergeant Lee and Sergeant Shade had any regular service; they were World War II combat veterans. Both of these sergeants assured us that we would be able to do as well as any mortar platoon once we had an opportunity to qualify as individuals and as a unit using live ammunition.

The train chuffed all night to Camp Lejeune. The ride was boring and hot. As the day began the Carolina sun took its toll. The jackets under our packs became soaked with perspiration as we marched from the train to a mess hall. We were late for morning mess and the cooks and messmen were in no mood to welcome us or serve us, for we were reservists, or citizen marines, and they were regulars—a distinction that they often brought to our attention.

Our company marched from the mess hall to a dock where we boarded a small ship and crossed the New River, which is about three miles wide at that point. We marched to a barracks at the rifle range where we would spend a week. Each man in our unit was required to qualify with the .30-caliber M-1 Garand rifle. Members of our mortar platoon had to qualify with the .45-caliber pistol. Most of the guys were very familiar with handling and shooting their own firearms but the range officers and personnel had their hands full teaching us how to shoot like Marines rather than shooting at squirrels, deer and rabbits. There was a lot of yelling as the regulars continuously reminded us to observe rifle range safety rules. We spent a day "snapping-in," or getting into each of the qualification shooting positions: sitting, standing and prone. The shooter would pull the trigger and upon hearing the snap of the firing pin his partner would whack the bolt back, simulating a round being fired and cocking the rifle for the next simulated firing.

We spent three days firing live ammunition at positions of 50 to 500 yards, and we did well. Everyone in the company qualified and many of us were awarded sharpshooter or distinguished marksman medals.

Staff Sergeant Lee's primary objective was that our mortar platoon would become qualified as a platoon, using live rounds, and our training at the Cumberland armory paid off on the mortar range. I found that I had an ability that I hadn't recognized, which was judging distances over various terrains. I was named acting leader of one of the three mortar platoon squads and we did exceptionally well firing the mortar.

We were not granted liberty from the base but there was a picnic at Onslow Beach. Field kitchens were set up and turned out great food. This was the first time most of us saw or swam in the ocean. There was plenty of beer available, but I didn't like the taste so I drank as much tonic as I could hold. Onslow Beach has dangerous rip tides and we were all challenged to swim in the surf. We started swimming at a point near a beach house and within a half hour the rip tide carried us hundreds of yards down the beach.

Two weeks at camp passed quickly and at the first reserve meeting after Camp Lejeune I was promoted to private first class. Our officers had a lot of praise for how well we did, especially since this was the first time a Marine unit from Cumberland had participated in an activity like that. They said our unit would be put through two weeks of advanced combat training next year as an amphibious landing unit.

Those two weeks spun through my mind during the remainder of the summer while I worked at the orchard. I mulled over the state of mind required to be a member of a killing force. The regular Marine personnel had made it very clear that we were all about hitting a target with as much destructive force as we had in our arsenal and keeping at it until nothing moved. Pictures of the destructive power created by the shells of our 60mm mortar flashed through my mind. Where the shells hit the ground there wasn't a blade of grass standing within about 25 yards. In an open mortar attack, if you weren't below ground you were a goner.

My Fort Hill High School 1949 senior class picture

Signs and banners welcomed the Senior Class of 1949 back to Fort Hill High. There was excitement about the coming year because our athletes in all sports were expected to "win it all." My class schedule was much lighter than my junior year and I was planning to attend all of the football and basketball games that I could.

I heard some guys talking about a 1917 Model T four-door sedan that was for sale for $25. I got the owner's name and that evening, with money in my pocket, I convinced Dad to take me by to see the car. The owner said the engine knocked and smoked and didn't have much power because it needed rings and rod bearings. He started it up by hand-cranking it. I said I'd take it and handed the man the $25. The owner said that it might not make it up the mountain until the engine was fixed. But I checked the radiator and it was full and the sight glass indicated that the gasoline tank was a quarter full, so I drove in front of Dad down Twiggtown Road toward the Millstone in a cloud of smoke. Things went well until I started up the grade near Mt. Tabor Church, when the engine quit. Dad pulled up alongside me and we checked things over. He suggested that the hill was so steep that the fluid level of the gas tank was lower than the carburetor;

hence, it wasn't getting fuel to the engine. I coasted backward down the mountain road to a place that was flat and we got the engine started. Then I drove backward up the mountain and the engine continued to run even at the steepest part. When I got home my neck had a crick in it from driving backward.

Overhauling the car was my fall and winter project. I ordered parts from the J. C. Whitney catalogue and began disassembling the engine, conferring often with others who had overhauled engines. I was able to borrow special tools such as torque wrenches and ring compressors and I replaced the piston rings, connecting rod bearings, transmission bands and drive-shaft brakes. I was ready for the maiden trip of my like-new 32-year-old car.

I invited Bill Reckley, Gladstone Beeler, and my nephew Herbie to be with me during this first outing. The new bearings caused the engine to be too tight to start it with the hand crank. I asked Dad to pull my car to the top of the hill near the cold storage shed. We'd let it coast down the grade above the house until the car had enough speed, then I would release the clutch to start the engine.

My scheme worked. We were coasting pretty well when I popped the clutch and the engine started—it sounded great! The guys were cheering and screaming and slapping me on the back as we rolled along. I adjusted the spark advance on the steering column and set the hand throttle, and the car was purring. Suddenly, the right rear side of the car heaved upward and Bill yelled, "Look at that wheel passing us!" The right rear of the car slumped down and Herbie began to scream at me. Meanwhile the car was fishtailing back and forth across the road and I couldn't control it and we ended up in the hay field in a cloud of dust.

Dad drove down to where we had stopped. We were jumping out of the car and fanning the dust off our faces. Dad was laughing and had tears making trails in the dust on his face. He said, "I've never seen anything so funny in all my born days. Your cheers became panic when the wheel came off."

Mom came running into the field and said, "Plumb my soul, I saw the wheel jump the road bank and land in the pigpen and it liked to have scared the pigs into a faint!"

I gathered my composure and rescued the wheel from the pigpen. Dad found the large wheel nut lying in the road where the wheel came off. All of us lifted the car and put blocks under the axle. I replaced the wheel and tightened the nut. This time I installed a cotter pin through the nut so that it would not come loose. The car started and we took joy rides around the mountain roads on the orchard for a couple hours. Everything was working fine.

Just before Thanksgiving a group of the guys from Sunday school decided to have a game of flag football in a pasture at Picnic Hollow after Sunday dinner.

This was a great opportunity to show off my car to some of the other Spring Gap guys and gals.

Herbie and I climbed into my car and we began descending the mountain for the first time. I was driving in high gear with the Rexhall gear engaged. The Rexhall gear was a freewheeling feature that allowed the wheels to turn directly proportional to the engine revolutions and gave the car more speed, but little power. It worked great on the flat and level where only minimum power was required. But little did I know that if the Rexhall gear became disengaged the transmission also was disengaged from the drive shaft to the rear wheels and neither the transmission brakes nor the gears would stop the car, for this car didn't have any front wheel brakes either.

Just below the high power line and before the 'S' curve the Rexhall gear disengaged and the car began careening down the mountain faster than I had ever driven. I was stepping on the brake, low gear, reverse; nothing worked! I even turned off the engine. Herbie was yell'n, "Slow down, you're going to kill both of us!" I decided to take immediate action by allowing the car to slide into the embankment and scrape hard against the bank until we stopped. I steered gently toward the right road bank and when the car began hitting the bank the bumper and fenders grabbed the dirt and rocks and the car spun around and we were going down the mountain backward. I had to steer in reverse to hold the left side against the bank. When we stopped we were covered with dust, gravel, clumps of sod and branches from the bushes we had hit.

My car was a mess; fenders on both sides were nearly ripped off the chassis. Herbie said, "You crashed here on the sled and just below here on the bicycle. If you get an airplane I'm not going to ride with you because we'll end up in the top of the trees at this same spot!" After I thought about what had happened, I concluded that I failed to pull the emergency brake. The emergency brake independently worked the brakes on the rear wheels. I became a pretty good body man as I repaired all the fenders and repainted the car using a paint brush.

One day on the school bus I struck up a conversation with a girl from Spring Gap, Barbara Jean. We had English class together. I figured I'd better start making sure I had a date for the prom, which was only six months off. I would be keeping Barbara Jean in mind.

Another afternoon, while I was in study hall, which consisted mostly of guys, we became unruly and were permanently suspended from attending that study hall. The school authorities determined that all of us would have to take a meaningful class and almost all of us chose typing. The typing teacher was a gentleman very small in stature. He immediately announced that we were the first all-male class he had ever taught and he believed that we could achieve better typing speeds and techniques than the females in one semester if we applied ourselves. Each guy took the challenge and we were off, working at achieving proficiency scores as high or higher than the girls. It appeared that I would achieve 50 words per minute at the end of the semester.

I now had something to talk to Barbara Jean about. She was a burner at the keyboard.

Mrs. Richtie assigned a major composition for English class. Due dates were established for various elements of the composition and we would be graded on each element. The outline element was due and I needed some help, so I asked Barbara Jean if I could work with her on the outline and we could evaluate each other's outline. We decided that we would meet at her house. She had three brothers, one older and two younger. I knew it was going to be difficult to put up with their teasing and mischief.

I arrived just as supper was over and the dishes had been put away. Barbara Jean and I began working on our homework in the living room and her brothers began their pranks and antics. Teen, Barbara's mother, scolded the boys and tried to keep them out of the living room but it didn't help much.

It was getting late and finally Barbara's brothers went to bed. Barbara was sitting on a small couch. She had her work spread out there and I was sitting on the floor, leaning against the couch and using the floor as a desk. We worked hard on the assignment. And we fell asleep.

I felt a nudge on my shoulder and heard Barbara's mother saying in a friendly tone, "Kenneth, I didn't know you were going to spend the night."

I looked up and asked, "What time is it?"

Teen replied, "It's 4:30 a.m."

I jumped up and gathered my things. Barbara's father was getting ready to have breakfast for he had to row a boat across the river to work at the B&O Railroad at Patterson Creek, West Virginia. I was shaking like a leaf for I expected him to really get after me. I said, "Good night, I mean morning!" and opened the kitchen door, stepped onto the porch in total darkness, and immediately stumbled over the dog who ran yelping and crying from the porch. Then in my startled condition I walked smack into the yard gate with a loud WHAM!

I hot-footed up the mountain in record time, worrying about what to say to Mom and Dad about being out all night. They would never believe my story about falling asleep. I expected to get the third degree. It was about 5:30 a.m. when I got home, the time when Mom generally began her day.

I entered the house, lifting up on the screen door as I opened it so that the hinges wouldn't squeak, and did the same for the main door, for it generally squeaked the worst. Mom wasn't in the kitchen. I opened the upstairs door and carefully dodged all the steps that made noise. I put my papers on the bureau and lay down in the bed with all my clothes on. I heard Mom rustling around downstairs, calling Dad to get up, and then she opened the door and called me to get ready for school. I couldn't believe that I had pulled it off. Neither Mom nor Dad knew that I had been out all night.

I wasn't very talkative in the car riding to the bus stop. Mrs. Miller was primed with current events but I couldn't think about current events. I was concerned about how embarrassed I would be when Barbara's brothers began teasing about spending all night with their sister. But, on the bus, the guys never mentioned the sleepover. It appeared the incident was being contained between Barbara's parents and the two of us. I received a passing grade on the composition outline, but I flunked my first "sort-of-a-date."

Some of my classmates were receiving college scholarships and our class president received an appointment to the U.S. Naval Academy. I had taken the Merchant Marine Academy examination and had received a letter explaining that the academy was interested in my application but wanted me to attend a maritime preparatory school for at least six months to improve on some academics and become familiar with academy expectations. The preparatory school would greatly improve my chances of acceptance. The bottom line was that attendance at the prep school would be at my expense. I forgot about that idea. And I didn't apply for scholarships offered by some teachers' colleges that required a commitment to teach school for two years, because I had decided I would not make a good teacher.

The prom was drawing near and it was only logical that I ask Barbara Jean to attend, and she accepted. The prom night about did me in from a money standpoint, getting a corsage, a suit and tie, and new shoes. Barbara Jean thought it would be fun to double-date and I arranged for us to pick up Eddie and Eileen. My sister Betty borrowed a big 1948 Cadillac convertible for me to use and I worried about how I would maneuver the narrow brick streets in Cumberland without scratching it.

Everyone had a wonderful time dancing and drinking punch in the school gym, which was decorated in a Hawaiian motif. It soon became obvious to me that we all would have been more comfortable in casual clothes. I got the car back to Betty without a scratch. I can't remember any conversations I had while driving it.

Mom and Dad gave me a 21-jewel Lord Baltimore Bulova watch and Betty gave me a Royal portable typewriter for graduation presents. I knew that Mom and Dad had spent a lot of money for the watch. My family was very proud that I was graduating.

I needed a plan. Most graduates who were not going to college were following a five-step one: get a job, purchase a car, marry their high school sweetheart, have kids, and buy a little house.

My Marine reserve unit departed for Camp Lejeune a couple of weeks after graduation. The summer maneuvers followed the same format as last year. The first five days were again at the rifle range but then the training changed drastically. We were introduced to an advanced combat training team. The trainers, wearing bright colored helmets, began giving us instructions on how to board a ship, perform an amphibious landing at Onslow Beach, and proceed to the target objectives.

When the order was given to go over the side of the ship and down a rope net into a landing craft, I almost froze. The team leaders were screaming at each man as he went over the side, in full combat gear. The only command that I heard clearly was to unhook my helmet chinstrap. I remembered from the briefing that if I fell into the ocean with the chinstrap hooked, the impact of the water under the helmet would break my neck. Somehow I was able to climb down the net, one foothold at a time, to the landing craft bobbing up and down and side to side about 40 feet below. Someone was holding the net so that I could scramble into the bouncing vessel. Smoke from the diesel engine was blowing directly into the hold and making many of us sick but I was able to hold everything in.

The landing craft circled in the open water for what seemed like an hour and then headed for the beach. This particular craft opened from the back and we were told that we would be jumping into two or three feet of water. We should run like hell for the beach, find cover, set up our three mortars in an appropriate position, and stand by for targeting information. Our landing marker would be a blue rectangle.

The landing craft bumped hard into the beach, knocking all of us onto our rear ends, and then the aft part of the craft opened and I was about the second person out. Instead of being in shallow water, it was nearly over my head. The rip tide was moving us down the beach when I saw a blue rectangular ground marker and headed for it. At about that time explosives hidden on the beach began going off, blowing sand everywhere. Six F4U Corsair aircraft came screaming across at about 50 feet altitude, adding to the excitement.

I was wet and covered with sand as I wallowed into a depression between some dunes. To my surprise all of my gun crew had made it to the same spot. We set up our mortar and placed a stake, which we used to aim the mortar shells. A second lieutenant wearing a colored helmet came up and gave specific targeting information and all three mortars soon were ready to fire. We didn't have ammunition for this exercise, however. It was a practice run.

When the landing exercise was over we assembled in an area that had bleacher seats. A colonel gave a short speech and commended us on our excellent deployment from the ship and our assembly as a Marine amphibious fighting unit. He noted that the mortar platoon made it ashore and was in an excellent position to support the riflemen and machine-gunners.

We loaded into trucks and began the long bumpy ride to barracks and a shower. I had learned something this first day: Amphibious landings aren't for the faint of heart.

At the end of the second week there was a formal parade and promotions were announced. I was promoted to corporal and made a squad leader.

Back home, I heard that some of the recent high school graduates were making 80 cents an hour in Washington, D.C., working as government clerks. That sure beat the 35 cents an hour I was making at the orchard. Since my sisters Lena, Betty and Georgia were living in an apartment in Washington, I wrote to inquire about coming to the city to look for work. Betty said that was fine with them as long as I didn't mind sleeping on a couch. She also wrote that Georgia was coming home on the bus and had someone to drive her back with all her belongings and maybe I could hitch a ride.

I had all my things ready as Georgia's friend came to pick us up. Mom was having a difficult time with things happening so fast. She, Dad and Herbie helped us load our belongings into a van and we were off. I hadn't really given much thought to leaving the mountain. I had planned my departure for so long, yet I never took time to recall how good it was growing up there. As we drove off the mountain I began to say to myself, "Goodbye, apple trees. Goodbye, power line. Goodbye, S turn and goodbye, MillStone." We headed toward Cumberland and Route 40, then east toward Hagerstown, Frederick and Washington, D.C.

My sisters' apartment was on Rhode Island Avenue NW near 14th Street. Lena and Georgia worked evenings at the Blue Mirror Lounge on 14th Street and

Betty worked days at an IGA grocery store. I began job-hunting by looking in the want ads and calling or going by to fill out applications. The government jobs would take about three months to get hired so I figured to take whatever I could get and if a government job came up I would go for it because the pay and benefits were much better.

The first opportunity that I had was with the Union Trust Company, working as a clerk-typist in their automobile finance department. It was ironic that they wanted someone who could type 40 words per minute, because my first job required a skill I had attained after being put out of a study hall in school. The starting pay was $32.50 for 40 hours. The manager requested that I wear a shirt and tie and if I went upstairs into the bank proper, wear a jacket. Betty helped me get a loan at a clothing store to purchase a suit.

I found a room at 1821 Biltmore Street NW. The rent was $20 a month for a room eight feet wide and twelve feet long, located in the basement of a former embassy building that had been converted into a rooming house. The room didn't have a window and the pipes running through the ceiling were noisy when the toilets in the upper levels were flushed, but it was my new home.

I enrolled at George Washington University, taking a three-credit course, College Algebra 101. Classes met for one hour on Monday, Wednesday and Friday nights. I wanted so badly to go to college that I was happy just to be taking three hours and working toward the required 120 hours to graduate. But my college classes directly interfered with the Marine reserve's Wednesday drill nights. I reported the conflict to my first sergeant and he informed me that most men had to change their class schedules in order to meet their drill commitments. As I was leaving the first sergeant's office he told me that there was a Marine reserve unit that met on weekends at the Anacostia Naval Air Station. On the following Saturday, I took the bus there, and guards at the gate directed me to a hangar where I met Master Sergeant Jack V. St. John. He said the unit was VMF-321, a Marine fighter squadron. He invited me to look around, and said that if I were interested he could have my records transferred and take steps to change my military occupational specification from infantry to aviation. The master sergeant introduced me to Staff Sergeant Buzz Aldrin, who showed me around the flight line. The airplanes were WWII era F6F Hellcats and F8F Bearcats. Buzz informed me that if I signed up with this unit I would be working for him and he would assign me responsibility for an airplane. My job title would be plane captain and my name would be stenciled on the side of the aircraft. I told Master Sergeant St. John to transfer my records and cut my orders to report at their next drill weekend.

As I boarded the bus back across to D.C., I couldn't believe my good fortune. I now had a great opportunity to learn aircraft mechanics and to fulfill my reserve obligations by working on airplanes. There was even a promise that I would receive "flight-skins," a $50 per quarter payment for four hours of flight time, although Master Sergeant St. John informed me that I shouldn't expect this bonus every quarter. I could hardly wait to begin getting in my flight time and receiving the extra pay.

My social life wasn't much because I had a full schedule of work, school and drill. I spent every penny that I was making. Most of my friends from home, including Barbara Jean, were working as clerks at the Justice Department, in the FBI fingerprinting and records sections. The government was hiring there because of the McCarthy investigations of Communist activities of hundreds of thousands of people.

City life was beginning to wear on me and I often thought about how good I had had it at home on Martins Mountain, where Mom prepared my meals in exchange for doing just a few chores. Although my salary was higher than at the orchard, my expenses for food, housing and transportation left me strapped for cash.

My sisters helped me with bus fare to go home at Christmas, and being home for a few days sure helped my homesickness. Mom and Dad made Christmas very special for me with the usual big dinner shared with my siblings and their families. Leaving home to return to the city was not as easy as when I had left for D.C. the first time.

I was offered a clerk-typist job at the FBI, working in the records section with my friends at a salary of $37.50 per week. The extra salary and benefits enticed me to accept the offer. It was customary for all new employees at the FBI to be introduced to J. Edgar Hoover, director of the FBI. As I shook his hand in his huge office I sensed an aurora of mystery and aloofness about him. He spoke a few words of welcome and disappeared through a door as special agents escorted us from his presence.

My job was to type on index cards the names and other information about individuals. My first assignment was to type out cards for Chinese individuals who had attended a conference in San Francisco. Each name required nine cards, listing the name in every possible combination. I needed a shopping cart to hold all the cards. Quotas were established for production of cards. Each completed job was sent to checkers and if they found any errors they returned the whole shopping cart.

Within three months after I began work at the FBI Records Section, North Korean forces invaded South Korea. The first news reports said that the President would have to call up reserves immediately. I couldn't believe that only five years after WWII, which had been a war to end all wars, and a mere one year after my graduation from high school, I would be faced with having to fight in a war. I was totally unprepared for being activated. Members of my unit received verbal orders to get our affairs in order so that we could be activated on short notice, and we got letters to give to our employers, colleges and any creditors. Barbara Jean and I had been dating regularly for about a month. The threat of my leaving for active duty was a shock for her. Within a few days the news came that my unit would be activated within 60 days, for operations at Anacostia Naval Air Station; Cherry Point, North Carolina; or El Toro, California.

Sister Betty borrowed a friend's 1949 Mercury convertible to help me to haul my civilian belongings back home to Spring Gap and I invited Barbara Jean to travel with us. We were crossing Copper Mountain on U.S. 50 about 20 miles from Romney, West Virginia, when Betty encountered glare ice as she was steering around a sharp curve. The car spun out of control, rolled twice, and ended up on its side. We were trapped inside. Passing motorists were able to open the car door from above, but we weren't able to climb out so they cut the canvas top to get us out. None of us was badly hurt; we had mostly bumps and scratches from the broken glass. The car was a total loss. We called my brother Tuck to come and help us home.

Barbara Jean and I caught a Greyhound bus back to Washington and Betty remained for an extra day to settle legal matters pertaining to the accident. While we were on the bus I asked Barbara Jean to accept my engagement ring, and she said yes.

The war news was terrible. Rumors and confusion were rampant within our unit at NAS Anacostia. To make things more intolerable, we were told that we would not be deployed as unit VMF-321 but as individuals. Men were disappearing without any fanfare or recognition as they received their orders. I searched the lists posted on the bulletin board and found my name. I was being transferred immediately to MCAS El Toro.

All was not well with me at El Toro, even though Kenneth Cage was stationed there and we would be able to buddy around together on liberty. We generally went skating at a skating rink in Costa Mesa. I was in a large maintenance squadron and I was essentially ignored for work assignments. It became apparent that this condition was not going to change. The units at El Toro were overstaffed due to the large number of reservists being called to active duty and the "good ol' boy" thing was evident in the selection of men to work on important assignments. Generally, I was only working half days. During the afternoons I had off, I worked on projects at the base hobby shops. I had ample free time so I made a two-holster western gun belt of the best top-grain leather. My hand-tooling was good enough that a Marine from Texas gave me $75 for it. The extra money helped, because I was having maximum deductions taken from my pay.

I asked my first sergeant about my prospects in the squadron, getting other assignments, or going to an engine school. He said that getting another outfit to take an interest in a transfer was out of the question. The engine schools were filled, primarily with higher-ranking men trying to get into the new jet-engine classes. I asked about GI Bill benefits and he said that only men that were actually in a combat zone would be eligible for the GI Bill.

"What's the chance of going overseas?" I asked.

He looked at me and said, "You want to go overseas?"

I responded, "If I can get the GI Bill, then I'm willing to go. What does it take to go overseas?"

He replied, "I can have you in Replacement Draft Number 9 tomorrow."

"Reassign me!" I blurted out.

He said, "Tomorrow, you report to the Replacement Barracks at 0600 hours."

He began filling out the paperwork and said, "I'll have your records over there at the Replacement Area tonight." Then he looked at me and said, "Congratulations, Sergeant Shipe."

Startled, I asked, "What do you mean, Sergeant Shipe?"

He showed me my records, which indicated I had been promoted, and said, "Going to Korea as a Marine sergeant will be a lot better for you, but it won't keep you out of harm's way."

The next day I was up early and reported at the Replacement Draft Area. I felt sick to my stomach as I stood in line at the sick bay, waiting to be inoculated with shots for my overseas assignment. I wasn't sick from the shots, but from dealing with the hasty decision I had made less than 24 hours earlier.

We could take a maximum five days leave to go home and I immediately scheduled a flight. As soon as I arrived in Washington, D.C., I unveiled a plan to Barbara Jean: We could get married right away but not live together until after I returned from overseas. We would save her allotment money and have enough to purchase a car, or we could apply the money toward tuition so that I could attend college fulltime on the GI Bill. After I had received my degree, I would be earning enough that she would be able to attend college fulltime.

Barbara Jean agreed to my plan and a justice of the peace in Rockledge, Maryland married us. The next day I flew from Washington National Airport back to El Toro. There, Jack St. John invited me to ride with him to Long Beach, where he was going to store his car until he returned from the Far East. We had to wait about four hours for a Greyhound back to El Toro and since we had some time we began walking around in Long Beach. Jack asked me to join him for a drink and we found a spot. The bartender said, "Since you guys are going overseas tomorrow, my specialty, a Zombie, is on me." I had never had a Zombie, but I said I'd try one. The bartender took his time and mixed the liquors so that they were layered and he held the drink to the light so that we could see the colors in his creation. The drink was a beauty. We had three of them. I began having difficulty walking and I was feeling sick so Jack and I walked to the beach and sat down. I felt real hot so I removed my shirt and lay on the sand. After about an hour Jack woke me and said, "The bus leaves in fifteen minutes. Put your shirt on and let's go!"

When I awoke in the barracks at 0500 hours on my last day in the States my head felt hollow, like an empty drum. Then I began to feel the pain from my sunburned, blistered back. I needed medication for my toasted skin. The guys around me informed me that if I reported to the sick bay I would be subject to court martial since we were under embarkation orders. Serious sunburn could be construed as a purposeful act to harm myself and escape from going overseas. I decided to tough it out.

Orders were given to "saddle up" and board a train that had been backed into the base near our barracks. As the train pulled out men were yelling and waving out the coach windows. The men on the base stopped their activities, waved and yelled, "Gung Ho!"

The train backed into the San Diego shipyard and we had about a ten-block march to the ship's gangway. My pack rubbed against my burning back and I wondered if I could tough it out. We stood for over an hour in the hot sun, waiting for our ship, the USNS General Black, a Liberty Class ship, to be loaded with Marines. Two other ships were being loaded with soldiers, airmen and sailors. Finally, we boarded the ship and were directed below to quarters on "C" deck. Our compartment was crammed with tiers of five canvas-bottomed sleeping racks suspended by chains from overhead. Each man was assigned a rack without regard to his choice; I ended up in the middle. The compartment was hot, the ventilation was poor, and the place smelled of diesel fuel. We had to stand by our assigned spot until all the Marines were aboard the ship. When we were allowed topside the sun was beginning to set and the ship was being prepared to sail. It appeared that every person on the ship was watching the rope lines being cast off from the dock and it was impossible to get to the rail. This was an indescribable moment, like no other in all my born days. I felt like the ship's lines were an umbilical cord, a lifeline. The words of my first sergeant about going into "harm's way" resounded in my thoughts for the first time. I was in a crowded mass of young men on the deck. I had always counted youth as strength; now I was dealing with the youthful inexperience of those around me to fight a war. I didn't know a soul. I couldn't keep my eyes from the expanse of water that grew wider between the ship and the shore.

The convoy of three troop ships formed three large Vs in the smooth harbor water. The setting sun shone a light orange in the wakes as the shoreline slipped down into the Pacific. Some of the men had tears in their eyes, straining to see the last harbor light flicker from the horizon. I didn't feel like crying; I was having trouble trying to absorb all that was happening. I stayed topside until the night air cooled, and I opened my jacket to allow the breeze from the ship's 15 knots to soothe my blistered back. As the voyage continued small groups of men gathered. We were all strangers; some of us made introductions and began talking about various things. The primary thing on each man's mind was the war and that we were heading toward one hell of a big fight. The scuttlebutt was that General MacArthur had been fired; the Marines had suffered their greatest losses in history as they were pushed from the Chosin Reservoir; and they were being evacuated from the port of Wonsan by ship and were preparing to regroup again in the Pusan Perimeter. The number of casualties, especially the KIA (killed in action) and MIA (missing in action), were higher than any U.S. war for the same period of time that the Korean War had been going on.

The ship's bell tolled once, signaling the beginning of the midnight watch, and I went below and climbed into my sack. My nose was about two inches from the bottom of the canvas of the sack above me. I closed my eyes and tried to sleep, but my mind was racing ninety to nothing, thinking about my situation. I concluded that my ambition to succeed as a man had caused me to push so hard on the door of opportunity that I had crashed it open; my momentum carried me through the door of opportunity and into the room of risk. I was scared. For the first time I realized that I had put my life in jeopardy by volunteering for combat duty, and whether I would come back was now a big, real "if." Each time I moved on the canvas sack the chains supporting the tier of racks made a noise. The chains were rattling throughout the compartment; I wasn't the only person having trouble sleeping. No longer were my eyes the only dry ones. I turned to the Lord and begged Him to hear my prayer. I told Him that I hadn't learned a better prayer like I had promised Him. I began to pray: "Now I lay me down to sleep and pray the Lord my soul to keep. If I should die before I wake, I pray the Lord my soul to take."

The ship's bell tolled eight bells, the end of the midnight watch. The Lord gave me peace about going into harm's way. I had concluded that I would be the best Marine that I could be. The term 'Gung Ho' began making sense for me, because it now meant that I had given my heart to God, and now my ass belonged to the Marine Corps.

15

To war and back

On the seventeenth day at sea, lying in my bunk, I could sense that the ship's screws were slowing. They slowed to a stop and I ran topside to see what was happening. The ship was in a fog bank, but I could see a couple of sampans illuminated by the yellowish light of the rising sun. The air carried a smell that I couldn't identify, except that it was foreign. As the fog began to lift I looked around for the two ships that had been with us but couldn't see them. They had gone to another port. I saw two tugboats plowing through the smooth water toward us, and soon they began to push us into port. The talk circulating among the men was that we were at the entrance to Tokyo Bay and we would be landing soon at Yokahama Naval Base.

I couldn't help thinking that six short years ago the Peace Treaty with Japan had been signed in this very harbor, aboard the USS Missouri, and at that time General Douglas MacArthur was one of the most famous military leaders in the world. Now President Truman had fired him and the situation in Korea couldn't be worse because a few months ago MacArthur had ordered the First Marine Division to race to the Yalu River, which separates North Korea from Manchuria, and to secure North Korea. The troops would be "home by Christmas," MacArthur said. But the Marines faced eight-to-one odds as Communist Chinese forces streamed out of Manchuria and drove the Marines and the U.S. Army X Corps out of North Korea. They were evacuated by ship from Wonsan, North Korea. Now the Marines were regrouping at the Pusan perimeter of South Korea, and we were to be their reinforcements.

The tugs shoved our ship toward the Yokahama dock. We could see evidence of damage to factories and warehouses that American bombers had inflicted in World War II.

Loudspeakers blared instructions for all hands to prepare to disembark. As we filed down a gangplank I struggled under the load of a pack, rifle, and sea bag. We marched directly to a waiting train and boarded. Within a few hours the train pulled out. It became obvious that this was a special train because it never slowed, even in cities, as we traveled all day and all night through Japan. I learned from the scuttlebutt, now my only source of information, that we were heading for Osaka, Japan's second largest city, situated on Honshu Island. We left the train at the Atami airbase, which during World War II had been the hotbed of Japanese kamikaze raids on our Pacific Fleet, and were assigned barracks. We were so exhausted that most of us fell onto a mattress without putting down sheets.

The next day we prepared to go to Korea. Our specific instructions listed what we could take with us: No identification other than dog tags, no photographs, no diary. The men in charge passed out large tags that we would clip onto our sea bags, onto which we wrote our names. The sea bags would remain in Japan. I suddenly realized that the only belongings and clothing I would have would be in my backpack.

My buddy, Ralph Moisner, had a 45-rpm record player in his pack instead of clothing. "Its more important to me to have my music than extra clothing," he explained. I volunteered to carry 12 of his records, all of them country western music. I had in my sea bag a 9 mm German Luger, which I switched to my pack so that I would have a personal sidearm.

Two days later, on the Atami tarmac, we shuffled aboard an R4Q transport plane, known as a flying boxcar, and within 90 minutes landed on a steel-matted airstrip at Mansan, South Korea. We stood in formation while officers read off names and the outfits we would be serving in. I was assigned to VMF (N)-513, also known as The Flying Nightmares. I threw my pack into the back of a jeep, which dropped me in front of a four-man tent that had a large number 36 on the wooden entrance door. This was my new home.

I got along well with the other three men in the tent. Soon I discovered that Ralph, the buddy with the 45-rpm record player, would be in my unit. We worked together on some of the first assignments such as putting lighted smudge pots beside the airstrip so planes could see the edge of the runway on take-offs and landings at night. We'd light the pots as the planes went off, and then snuff them out until the planes returned. We did this so that enemy spotters couldn't pinpoint where we were located.

As the days passed the Chinese forces surprised us by not continuing down the Korean peninsula and trying to push the weakened United Nations forces into the sea, as had been expected. So we began an operation formally known as the United Nations Counteroffensive. Our first sergeant asked for volunteers to go north and help prepare an airfield for use by our unit and also work as spotters to communicate ground-to-air instructions to the planes as required to hit vital targets. I said I'd be interested, and so would my buddy, Ralph. Then I ran down the flight line and told Ralph that we were going to a base in North Korea, K-50, and he should be ready by 9 the next morning. Ralph was incredulous. Despite my attempts to convince him that it would be a great adventure he couldn't believe that I had volunteered him.

An R4D-8 two-engine transport plane took us nearly 200 miles north, landing at K-18 airstrip near a beach on the Sea of Japan. We disembarked to find only four tents set up and Seabees throwing other tents off a truck. One tent was ours, they said. We were told to report to Captain Ball. Unfortunately, no one knew the captain or where to find him. We ate chow with the Seabees and hung around three or four days until I decided to find the First Marine Division headquarters. There we located the missing captain. He didn't have an assignment for us in his close air support unit, but he put me in charge of a detail that would prepare a beach for landing supplies from LST ships. "You're going to remain at K-18," he told me. I should commandeer a jeep from some unit and drive about 18 miles each day up to Chumanjin. There Ralph and I and 14 other men would prepare a beach so that ships could come in with supplies. Soon, LSTs were landing at our beach, opening their cavernous bow doors, and lowering their ramps to unload supplies. Often as many as three ships were unloading at a time, and huge stocks of munitions and other supplies were piled along the beach. After a while Captain Ball negotiated with a Republic of South Korea (ROK) Army unit to take over the activities at Chumanjin, and we were relieved of that part of our duty.

Ralph and me, eating "C" rations at Chumanjin, Korea (K-50)—1951

After about two months our unit, VMF (N)-513, arrived at K-18. Ralph and I rejoined the squadron and its operations. The squadron had two different types of aircraft, F4U-5N Corsairs and F7F-3N Tigercats, which was an unusual circumstance caused by heavy losses of aircraft. One of the reasons for the losses was that the Chinese Communist Forces stretched cables across the narrow valleys, and placed lights on the roads below the cables. The lights appeared from the air to be military trucks and tanks. The cables didn't show on radar and our night fighters flew into them in the dark. Many planes were lost. One night, Major Redmond returned to base in his Tigercat with only one engine operating. About 150 feet of cable was wrapped around the dead engine. The loose ends nearly whipped the tail section of his plane to shreds.

The radar-equipped planes in our squadron were the remainder of two night-fighter squadrons, VMF (N)-513 and VMF (N)-542. The full compliment of aircraft for two squadrons would have been 48 aircraft but we only had 18 planes total.

The weather was turning cold. What little winter clothing we had was in Japan, so our supply sergeants did midnight requisitions from Army and Air Force units. We kept warm wearing multiple layers of nice wool Army officers' dress shirts and pants. Why the marines were not issued heavy winter work clothing, I could never understand. Perhaps the "brass" was still thinking about the South Pacific.

The hard winter weather of 1951 in Korea made living in the field miserable. Just before Christmas a 30-inch snowstorm halted all operations for a full two-and-a-half weeks. I was promoted to staff sergeant and the good feeling about the promotion helped me endure the terrible conditions of working and living in tents in sub-zero weather. We endured one-week of minus 30 degrees. My shoes were leather low-cut, "boondockers." I wrapped my feet with newspaper to help keep them warm; it was something I often did during winters back home on Martins Mountain.

One night, Ralph and I heard a scratching sound on the front flap of our tent. Ralph opened the flap and I heard a familiar voice saying, "Is Kenneth Shipe from Spring Gap here?"

I yelled, "Who knows I'm from Spring Gap?"

Kenneth Cage, my best friend from home, entered the tent and we hooted and hollered as we expressed our disbelief that we were together again under these circumstances and conditions. He told us about what he had been doing and said he was a radioman in a fighter squadron stationed across the airfield here at K-18.

We caught up on news from home. He had been back to Japan on R&R, after his squadron came off aircraft carrier duty, and he had some souvenirs that he wanted to show me.

Kenneth Cage and me in front of the "Checkerboard Squadron" flight line at K-18—1951

The next day, as I was walking near the "Checkerboard Squadron" flight line, on my way toward Kenneth's tent to see his souvenirs, the emergency siren sounded. I looked down the runway and saw a Navy AD-3 Skyraider aircraft coming in. The plane had a serious landing gear problem; only one wheel was lowered. This type of emergency was a daily happening at this forward air base. Not only were crippled Marine, ROK, and Air Force aircraft making emergency landings, but Navy aircraft that were too damaged to land aboard their carriers also were directed to land at K-18.

As the crippled Skyraider's wheel touched down the landing gear collapsed and the plane careened off the runway, tumbling and gouging the ground, breaking apart as it cart-wheeled toward the flight line and me. It was hard to determine which direction I should run for safety. Large parts from the plane were slamming into the parked and fully loaded fighter planes on the line. The cockpit section of the crashing aircraft separated from the engine, wings, rear section and tail section. There was a tremendous explosion at the flight line. The cockpit skidded to a stop about 40 yards from me and I saw the pilot unbuckle his harness and begin running from the wreckage, bent over and limping badly as he scrambled. An ambulance picked him up. The explosions began and everyone was running away. Exploding napalm bombs and 20mm cannon ammunition filled the sky. Shrapnel was whizzing by my head and raining down around me. Marines were yelling that the burning planes were each loaded with 500-pound bombs. A black soldier jumped onto a bulldozer and, using the blade as a shield, pushed five burning airplanes away from those that were not burning. Later he was decorated with a Silver Star for bravery.

Kenneth was out there on the flight line. He later described how when the plane crashed he had helped a pilot out of the cockpit and was running toward the beach when the pilot, despite the handicap of a big parachute slapping him on the back of the legs, outran him to safety.

During the crash I was beside the runway when the plane hit about 100 yards down the tarmac. The engine rolled in front of me, about 50 feet away, knocking down tents as it went. Live ammunition was exploding and the shells were cutting telephone and electric lines. Running away from the fiery scene, I stepped into what probably was a foxhole or post-hole. One leg went down into the hole, the other stayed on top. My back was injured so that I couldn't get out of the hole on my own. Medics took me to a field hospital and applied heat and compresses for three days, until I could walk and return to duty. I think that was when I ruptured a disc.

Christmas, 1951, was not a joyous time for the marines at K-18. The Communist propaganda radio featured the voice of a woman, P'yongyang Sally, who was predicting that our Christmas gift was going to be a bombing raid on our base and a bomb for each man. She had the name of our commanding officer, as well as names of the commanding officers of every squadron at K-18. She said none of the people at K-18 would ever celebrate another Christmas. There were plenty of rumors that the Russians had not only supplied the North Koreans with MIG fighters, but also bombers. The propaganda was working, for we were very edgy.

We were all at a heightened state of alert and very jumpy. Our guys were nervous and were not taking any chances. This became evident one night as one of our aircraft was returning from a mission. His IFF (identification friend or foe transmitter) had failed and the early warning system operators didn't know who he was. The anti-aircraft batteries at the base opened up, trying to shoot the plane out of the sky, but he was able to turn away unharmed. The agitated pilot radioed the tower asking, "What in hell is going on?" The tower informed him that his IFF was inoperative. The pilot gave his call letters and tail number for proper identification, and was given clearance to land.

When I heard the ack, ack of cannons firing and the explosions overhead I rolled out of my sack through the tent flap and into a foxhole that I had dug on the outside edge of the tent. Believe me, I wasn't the only Marine that hit his fox-hole that night.

My primary job was crew chief leader, responsible for the flightworthiness of our F4U-5N Corsairs to perform their night missions, but almost nightly I had been requesting to fly on any combat mission in the radar operator's position aboard one of our F7F-3N Tigercat aircraft. On one cold, dark night in January 1952, the ready room informed me that Lieutenant Andre's radar operator was ill and that the mission on this particular night did not require an RO. I climbed into the RO cockpit and strapped the parachute harness around me, then pulled the shoulder straps down and snapped them into the seatbelt buckle. I had flown many hours in this position in order to earn my monthly flight pay. The red instrument panel lights illuminated the compartment enough that I could verify where the major components were located in the cockpit in the event of an emergency.

Lieutenant Andre started the two 2800-horsepower Pratt and Whitney engines one at a time and they belched fire and smoke from the exhaust stacks. We were ready for the wheel chocks to be removed, which normally was my job as a ground crewman. We received the customary salute from the ground crew and taxied to the end of the strip. The tower operator signaled with a green light that we were cleared for takeoff. Lieutenant Andre released the brakes and the sleek Tigercat sped down the runway, and into the black winter sky.

Soon, we were crossing the bomb line into enemy-held territory. Lieutenant Andre radioed a ground check station using his aircraft call identification: "Coffee Grinder, this is Willie Foxtrot 21." The ground station acknowledged the mission we were flying and relayed coordinates for the position of the P2V-4 Navy patrol aircraft, which were the watchful eyes that located targets for our nightfighters to swoop down low and destroy.

As we proceeded toward the target area, Singosan Valley, a major supply route near Wonsan, Lieutenant Andre informed me over the intercom that he would fire a short burst from the 20mm cannons mounted inside both wings. The tracer bullets were the only light outside our aircraft in the pitch-black sky.

Lieutenant Andre established communications with the Navy aircraft crew and they told him that they had seen a few momentary flashes of light on the ground, a good indicator that a convoy was below and using minimum lighting. The Navy aircraft dropped a couple of flares and the valley and one side of a mountain lit up like noonday. There, on a road along the side of the mountain, were a dozen enemy trucks, most of them fuel tankers.

Lieutenant Andre advised me that he had armed his bomb racks and to make ready for action. He banked the aircraft sharply, dove toward the target, and fired a couple of rockets at the last truck in the column. Making a second pass, he fired more rockets at the lead truck. We were turning and twisting in the air when he dropped two 100-pound fragmentation bombs. He had many trucks on fire but the fires weren't anything compared to what was to come next. He strafed the lead truck and the burning contents of two or three fuel trucks began running down the road, igniting truck after truck. The display of fire and explosions was the most destruction I had ever seen in all my born days.

Lieutenant Andre made a couple passes to verify that all of the targets were destroyed, and as best that I could tell they were all on fire.

Back at our base, I climbed out of the Tigercat and congratulated the lieutenant on his fine piece of night flying and the successful kills. I tried to express my appreciation for the experience of flying this mission.

My buddies wanted to know about the mission, and how it felt to be on a raid. I told them, "Lieutenant Andre made it all happen. You ground crews should be proud that your efforts, mixed with the lieutenant's skill and bravery, translates into the fact that a dozen trucks and their cargo will not reach their destination tonight in support of some 'gook' effort to kill marines."

The months I spent in Korea, working on the flight line and getting supplies from the beach to the base, matured me. I arrived a 19-year-old youth and left as a mature young man. At first I was always aware of being at extreme risk all the time. But after a while I got used to that feeling and sleeping ceased to be a problem. I felt good about being in the war, and I knew that I was contributing to a larger effort. Yet, I began to think only about my little day-to-day piece of that effort, knowing that I had no control over the situations that we faced. The things I had learned in Spring Gap were valuable to me. Growing up on a farm without electricity had prepared me for survival in a tent during the cold winter. I was used to getting by with little and not being concerned about starving or freezing, as were some of the men who came from cities. Some of them were afraid of the dark but it didn't much bother me, because that was what nights had been like in Spring Gap.

The time approached when I was going on R&R. Thinking that Japan would be warm in April, I removed my woolen garments and wore my light marine jacket, trousers and underwear for the flight to Itami Air Base in Japan. But it was unusually cold in Japan and I came down with chills, a high fever, and a sore throat. The U.S. Army operated a dispensary in the Nara Hotel, where I was assigned for R&R. The doctor on duty there painted my throat with tincture of purple, gave me a handful of aspirin, and advised three days of bed rest. The cold weather and illness spoiled my R&R plans. I was able to do a little shopping in Osaka but missed out on sightseeing in Nara, the ancient capitol of Japan.

The Panmunjon Peace Talks had begun but the fighting became more intense instead of subsiding. The Chinese Communist Forces used the peace talks to hide their offensive intentions, a fact that impacted the plans of men like myself waiting to rotate back to the U.S.

Our unit had lost so many aircraft that we were barely able to perform our mission. We were using World War II-era planes and headquarters was not replacing them. We had six F4U5Ns and four F7F3Ns instead of the 24 aircraft allotted to a normal squadron. Rumors that our unit would return to Japan, or even back to the States, were false. Instead, we were deployed to an airfield close to Kunsan, near the Yellow Sea and south of Seoul. This base was designated as K-8, and the airfield was shared with Air Force Squadrons flying B-26 bombers. This deployment took us from the east coast of Korea to the west coast.

The twin missions of VMF(N)-513 were to continue night interdiction raids against Chinese Communist Forces in North Korea, and to fly "night cap" missions in and around Seoul, especially over the huge Air Force base at Kimpo, designated as K-13. These latter missions were necessary because Air Force F-94s were unable to use their all-weather, radar-equipped jet fighters to go after the slow North Korean propeller-powered biplanes that were harassing the operations at K-13. The F-94's couldn't shoot at the North Korean planes because they couldn't fly slowly enough to avoid over-running the slower craft or stalling out. The North Koreans flew between the mountains, at treetop level, and below radar detection, and threw hand grenades or mortar rounds onto the airbase before racing at their top speed of 110 mph for home. The Marine Corsairs and Tigercats could shoot down the enemy planes only by flying slowly, using flaps to reduce their airspeed, and maneuvering behind the enemy to blast them out of the sky with 20mm cannons.

Many of us were counting the days until we thought we would be rotated back to the States. According to my plan I would be a civilian, at home, back at my FBI job and registered in college for the 1952 fall semester. Since my tour of duty in Korea was in a combat zone I was sure of having four years of GI Bill eligibility. My name appeared on the May list for returning stateside. On May 15, with orders in hand, I put on my backpack and headed for the tarmac to catch the mail plane back to Japan. As I passed the bulletin board, a marine was posting a notice. It announced that all transfers were frozen, 'at the convenience of the government," which meant that I was going nowhere.

The reason given was that the North Koreans had walked out of the Panmunjon peace talks. Rumors ran rampant among the troops about when we would be going home—everything from six-month to one-year extensions. Some rumors had us in an all-out war with China. Only when I was boarding the troop transport ship, the USNS General William Weigle, bound for San Francisco with 5,500 other men, did I believe the Korean War was behind me and I was on my way back home.

Military records state that my release from active duty was on July 7, 1952 in San Diego. My physical examination records show my height as 72 inches, my weight 128 pounds, with gray eyes, brown hair, and a ruddy complexion.

Me after return from Korea—1952

With some of my mustering-out pay I purchased an airline ticket to D.C. and I had $143 remaining in my wallet. After attending a movie the evening before my flight I discovered that my wallet was missing. I rushed back to the theater and an usher helped me search for the missing wallet. Using her flashlight she looked around where I had been seated and found the wallet wedged between the seat hinge and the cushion. Nothing was missing. I immediately purchased a new wallet, one that wouldn't slip out of my front pocket when I sat down. Marine trousers did not have hip pockets.

Barbara Jean met me at Washington International Airport with keys to a new 1952 Pontiac Catalina hardtop convertible. I inquired about plans for a honeymoon and whether she had her bags in the car, and she informed me that she was unable to schedule a vacation from her job at the FBI. She suggested that I take the car and drive to Spring Gap, and she could ride the bus the following weekend to join me.

While visiting at Spring Gap my nephew, Eugene Shipe, who was Clyde and Hazel's only son, drowned in a farm pond near Centerville, Pennsylvania. His funeral was the first time we could recall that all ten members of my immediate family were together as adults.

Barbara Jean didn't come to Spring Gap, as she had promised. I drove back to D.C. and confronted her about her indifference toward me. One conversation led to another and nothing was getting resolved. We concluded that our differences could not be reconciled and that our marriage should be annulled. Within a week the court proceedings were over, and four weeks later the annulment was final.

Photo of my immediate family taken after Eugene Shipe's funeral—1952
L to R, top row: Herbert, Dad, Mom, Clyde; middle row: Jesse, me and William;
bottom row: Lena, Georgia and Betty

I resigned my job at the FBI, re-enlisted in the marines for a three-year hitch, and returned the unpaid-for Pontiac to the dealer, who worked out an arrangement for me to purchase a 1949 Pontiac coupe. My orders were to report for duty at the USMC Air Station at Opa Locka, Florida, by September 2, 1952.

Driving south on U.S. 1 toward Florida, my mind was busy with a lot of soul-searching and "what ifs." All of my plans had backfired and I was angry and disappointed with myself. Sometime around two in the morning, somewhere between Quantico and Richmond, Virginia, I pulled off the highway at a Shell gasoline station and tried to rest.

At daybreak I used the restroom at the station. The attendant was changing the oil in a car and we struck up a conversation. His name was Bob, and he was a former marine. He listened to my story about my failures. Using a shop rag, he wiped oil and grease from his hands and pulled a map of the Eastern United States from the rack. He ran his finger down the map to Florida, and we both began looking for Opa Locka. We agreed that a new Marine base would be somewhere in a Florida swamp, for generally that's where Marine bases on the East Coast were located. Bob yelled, "There it is, and my Lord, look! It's right on the outskirts of Miami and just west of Miami Beach!

"I think you are the luckiest Marine in the world. I can't feel sorry for you anymore, man! You're single, twenty years old, a Marine staff sergeant, and you have a contract for three years in paradise! If I were you, I would have my ass in my car and scratching south on U.S. 1 like a scalded dog!"

Bob slapped the top of my car with his big hand and said, "Drive safely and 'Semper Fi!"

I pulled back onto U.S. 1 heading south and yelled out the car window, "Semper Fi!"

16

My family origins

A preacher by the name of Casper Scheib, a fifteenth great-grandfather of mine, came to Odernheim am Glan, County of Bad Kreusnach, Rheinland-Pfalz Territory, Germany to be the pastor of the church there in 1584. Casper was born in 1560, and he was pastor in Odernheim until his death in 1631.

Casper's grandson, Valentin Scheib, was born in 1701 in Odernheim am Glan and visited the American colonial city of Philadelphia on September 23, 1732, aboard the ship *Adventurer*, mastered by Robert Carson. The ship was from Rotterdam and the last port was Cowes, England. Records show that he did not stay in America. Documents indicate that when his will was processed in Germany, dated August 23, 1769 it dealt with the estate of the citizen and master shoemaker Valentin Scheib of Odernheim, and said he died about four weeks ago. The record also states that he had a son from his first marriage, Christian Scheib, and this son was living in America. Records confirm that Valentin died July 23, 1769.

Valentin's son, Christian Scheib, arrived in Philadelphia in September 1751 aboard the ship *Edinburgh*, mastered by Captain James Russell. In 1751 all ships carrying German immigrants were required to dock at Philadelphia and all German immigrants were required to take the oath of allegiance to the Crown of England upon the very day of their arrival.

Christian Scheib began his life in the New World in Northampton, Pennsylvania, one of five towns in Pennsylvania that had many 'plain people' living on land grants from a vast acreage originally purchased from the King of England by William Penn, a Quaker leader for whom Pennsylvania (Penn's woods) was named. William Penn later divided and sold the land to individual immigrants. The people in Germany knew about the land grants because Penn had advertisements printed in German and posted in many German cities. He also visited Germany at least three times to spread his message.

Christian Scheib and many like him were referred to as German Pietists, or Brethren. Several Anabaptist groups have used the word "Brethren." The word Anabaptist means "adult baptisms"—people who believe that only adult believers can be baptized for salvation, and then and only then are they candidates for church membership.

I learned more about the Anabaptists from an article in *Family Chronicle* magazine entitled, "Strangers in His Majesty's Colonies: The History of the German Pietists," written by Richard L. Hooverson. He wrote that these Brethren groups have markedly different histories but many share similar religious beliefs or practices. A few of these groups are the Moravians, the Anabaptists, the Mennonites, the Palatines, the Dunkards, the Seventh Day Baptists, the Schwenckfelders and the Moravian Brethren.

The ruling princes in Germany persecuted and put to death many of the people in Anabaptists religious groups because they also did not believe in a state church for the masses or swearing allegiance to anyone but God.

The Brethren called their ministers from within their own congregations, preached that the Bible was the only source for God's Word, and emphasized inner moral perfection, a spirit that was later embraced by the English Quakers and in the Methodism that grew out of the Anglican Church here in America.

The people who left their homes in Germany and settled in Pennsylvania found it wasn't long until they heard rumblings that would impact their lives. As early as 1727, when the German population in Pennsylvania numbered about 20,000, the governor referred to them as "strangers to His Majesty's colonies." During the Revolutionary War most German 'church people' supported the rebellion; however, the Quakers, Mennonites, and Brethren, our nation's three historic peace churches, were pacifist.

The Great Church Awakening, which spanned the Revolutionary War, shook the established churches and set in motion forces that caused American religion to become forever different from the Old World model. This spiritual resurgence was said by many to have been ignited by the Presbyterians, spread by the Baptists, and matured by the Methodists. George Whitfield, an Anglican from Oxford and an associate of John and Charles Wesley, made seven visits to the Colonies between 1739 and 1769, and he preached from New England to Georgia. His hellfire and damnation style became the model for later 'revivals' and drew many ministers to a renewed vision.

After the Revolutionary War the Pennsylvania Legislature required its citizens to swear allegiance to the Commonwealth of Pennsylvania. Most 'plain people,' disdaining oaths and resisting violence, refused to do so. Many suffered fines, abuse, and public censure and some sold their lands and moved to new locales including western Virginia and western Maryland along the Braddock Trail, where government influence was scarce. The American Revolution confirmed the principle of separation of church and state, a right that the German Pietists had long cherished.

Christian Scheib bought land in Frederick County, Virginia, in 1773 and then sold the land in 1774; his wife Anna Maria also signed the deed. There isn't any evidence of why he only held the land for one year. Exactly how long he stayed in Virginia is not certain, but it is speculated that he spent at least fifteen years there before moving back to Northhampton, Pennsylvania where he died on May 31, 1794. During these times the United Brethren Church (UBC) was formed—a Methodistic "mini-Reformation" within the German Reformed Church. It is very likely that Christian was active in these church movements.

The family name, Scheib, is pronounced in German as "Shi pee", for the 'b' is pronounced as a 'p', and it probably came to be spelled Shipe for two possible reasons: First, because the family became tired of the English census-takers and others misspelling their family name. Few of the Germans could read or write English; hence, the census takers wrote the name as it sounded. Second, because the family would not swear allegiance to the Commonwealth of Pennsylvania or Virginia so they had to move on into the Allegheny mountain area to avoid persecution, and they changed their name to be more English so that they might be left alone to practice their beliefs.

Christian's son, Christian Scheib/Shipe, Jr. was born about 1760 in Pennsylvania. He married Anna Cryzer on December 21, 1785, in Shenandoah County, Virginia. He and his wife are listed on the reconstructed 1790 census of Virginia as being in Frederick County. In the 1810 Virginia census he is listed as Christian Shipe, Jr. and lived in Shenandoah County, Virginia. (Here is an interesting bit of family history: One of Christian Jr's sons, John Shipe, is my paternal great-great-grandfather and another son, Isaac Shipe, is my maternal great-great-grandfather.) I am not my own grandpa, but I am double related and my own fifth cousin.

Following along my father's line of descendants, we find that John Shipe had a son, Joseph Shipe, born in 1827, who settled in the Lost River area near Mathias, Hardy County, Virginia. After his marriage to Nancy Darr they had a son, Lorenzo Dale Shipe, in 1856. Lorenzo is my paternal grandfather. I found that the West Virginia/Virginia boundary line of today runs between the barn and house that Lorenzo built. This home is located in the former Dovesville section of the Lost River area in Hardy County.

Following down my mother's line of descendants, I found that Isaac Shipe had a son, John William Shipe, the third child of Isaac and Mary Shipe, who settled in Horseshoe Run, Mineral County, Virginia. John William was born in January 1834, in Shenandoah County, Virginia. He first appears on the 1850 Census in Frederick County, Virginia, living there with his parents. On July 14, 1861, three months after the outbreak of the Civil War, he joined the Virginia Militia in Romney, Virginia (now West Virginia), and was assigned to company A, 77th Regiment of the Virginia Cavalry. The 77th Regiment Virginia Militia was called out by proclamation of the Governor of Virginia dated July 13, 1861.

On April 1, 1862, John William joined Company D, 7th Regiment, Virginia Cavalry (also known as "Ashby's Cavalry"), and is shown on muster rolls for the months of November and December. On December 23, 1862, John is noted as having deserted in New Market, Virginia. As to why he chose to leave at this time is uncertain. Perhaps it had something to do with Turner Ashby's death in May of that year. But, perhaps the most compelling reason, and one that requires minimal speculation, is that Virginia seceded from the Union in 1861. Western counties objected. Fifty western counties united to form 'The Restored Government of Virginia' and petitioned the U.S. Congress for re-admittance to the Union. The state of West Virginia was admitted to the Union in 1863, after Union victories in the area cleared out the Confederates.

On October 14, 1863, John, whose home is now in Union territory, enlisted with Company D, 15th Regiment, Virginia Infantry. He had to travel to Luray, Virginia, to re-enlist. John remains on the Company muster rolls for the remainder of the war. From August 19, 1864 through December 10, 1864, he was in Chimborazo Hospital #2 in Richmond, Virginia, suffering from a fever. He appears back on the rolls for the rest of the war. On April 26, 1865, in Winchester, Virginia, he signed an oath of allegiance swearing that he would not take up arms against the United States Government, would conduct himself as a peaceful and honorable citizen, and would do nothing to the detriment of the United States Government. On this deposition, he was described as about 5 feet 10 and one half inches in height, of fair complexion, with light brown hair and gray eyes.

After the war, John William lived in the Mineral County and Hampshire County areas of West Virginia. In the later part of the 1800s, the family was living around a town named Alaska (now Keyser, West Virginia). Their oldest child, Bettie, died of consumption on December 18, 1888, and his wife, Margaret White Shipe, died on August 6, 1897. She was buried in Queen's Point Cemetery in Keyser. Her son Isaac obtained her grave plot.

Soon after his wife's death, John William Shipe was willed land from his brother, John E. Shipe and with his son, John David, took up farming on this property, which soon became known as Horseshoe Run. John William's failing health required him to turn the property over to John David and his wife. (John David Shipe is my maternal grandfather.)

John William Shipe died in 1913. It was a very bad winter and on February 2, Groundhog Day, his body was taken by horse-drawn wagon in axle-deep snow to be buried in Mount Zion Cemetery in Fountain, West Virginia. The divisive issues from the Civil War continued to impact John William, even in death, for after his death his family was forbidden to bury him in Queen's Point Cemetery next to his wife. At that time a lawsuit was pending prohibiting Confederate veterans from burial in public cemeteries in Keyser, West Virginia.

My mother, Pearl Amanda Shipe, is the daughter of John David Shipe and Samantha Lee Fleek of Keyser, West Virginia. My mother's people were 'shouting, hanky-waving Methodists.' These families farmed the valleys and worked the mountain orchards in the Knobly Mountains and along Patterson's Creek, known as Horseshoe Run, near Fort Ashby in Mineral County, West Virginia.

My father, John Russell Shipe, is the son of Lorenzo Dale Shipe and Matilda Cullers of Mathias, Hardy County, West Virginia. My mother told me that my father's people were, 'plain people'—farmers who dressed in pants and dresses held together with pins instead of buttons or snaps. The women covered their heads with bonnets and the men wore hats when outdoors. Generally, the men wore beards but not mustaches; they were German Brethren.

0-595-28795-6

www.ingramcontent.com/pod-product-compliance
Lightning Source LLC
Chambersburg PA
CBHW020913290526
45784CB00002BA/535